GRAPHIC HISTORY

THE BUILDING OF THE TRANSCONTINENTAL RAILROAD

by Nathan Olson

illustrated by Richard Dominguez
and Charles Barnett III

Consultants:
Bob and Julie Lettenberger
National Railroad Museum
Green Bay, Wisconsin

Capstone
press®

Mankato, Minnesota

Graphic Library is published by Capstone Press,
1710 Roe Crest Drive, North Mankato, Minnesota 56003.
www.capstonepub.com

Books published by Capstone Press are manufactured with paper
containing at least 10 percent post-consumer waste.

Library of Congress Cataloging-in-Publication Data
Olson, Nathan.
   The building of the transcontinental railroad / by Nathan Olson; illustrated by Richard
Dominguez and Charles Barnett III.
   p. cm.—(Graphic library. Graphic history.)
   Includes bibliographical references and index.
   ISBN-13: 978-0-7368-6490-9 (hardcover)
   ISBN-10: 0-7368-6490-3 (hardcover)
   ISBN-13: 978-0-7368-9652-8 (softcover pbk.)
   ISBN-10: 0-7368-9652-X (softcover pbk.)
   1. Pacific railroads—Juvenile literature. 2. Railroads—United States—History—Juvenile
literature. I. Title. II. Series.
TF25.P23O56 2007
385.0973—dc22   2006008309

Summary: In graphic novel format, tells the story of how the Transcontinental Railroad was built
   during the 1800s.

Designer
Bob Lentz

Production Designer
Kim Brown

Colorist
Buzz Setzer

Editor
Donald Lemke

Printed in the United States of America in Stevens Point, Wisconsin.
082012
006899

TABLE of CONTENTS

CHAPTER 1

A CRAZY IDEA

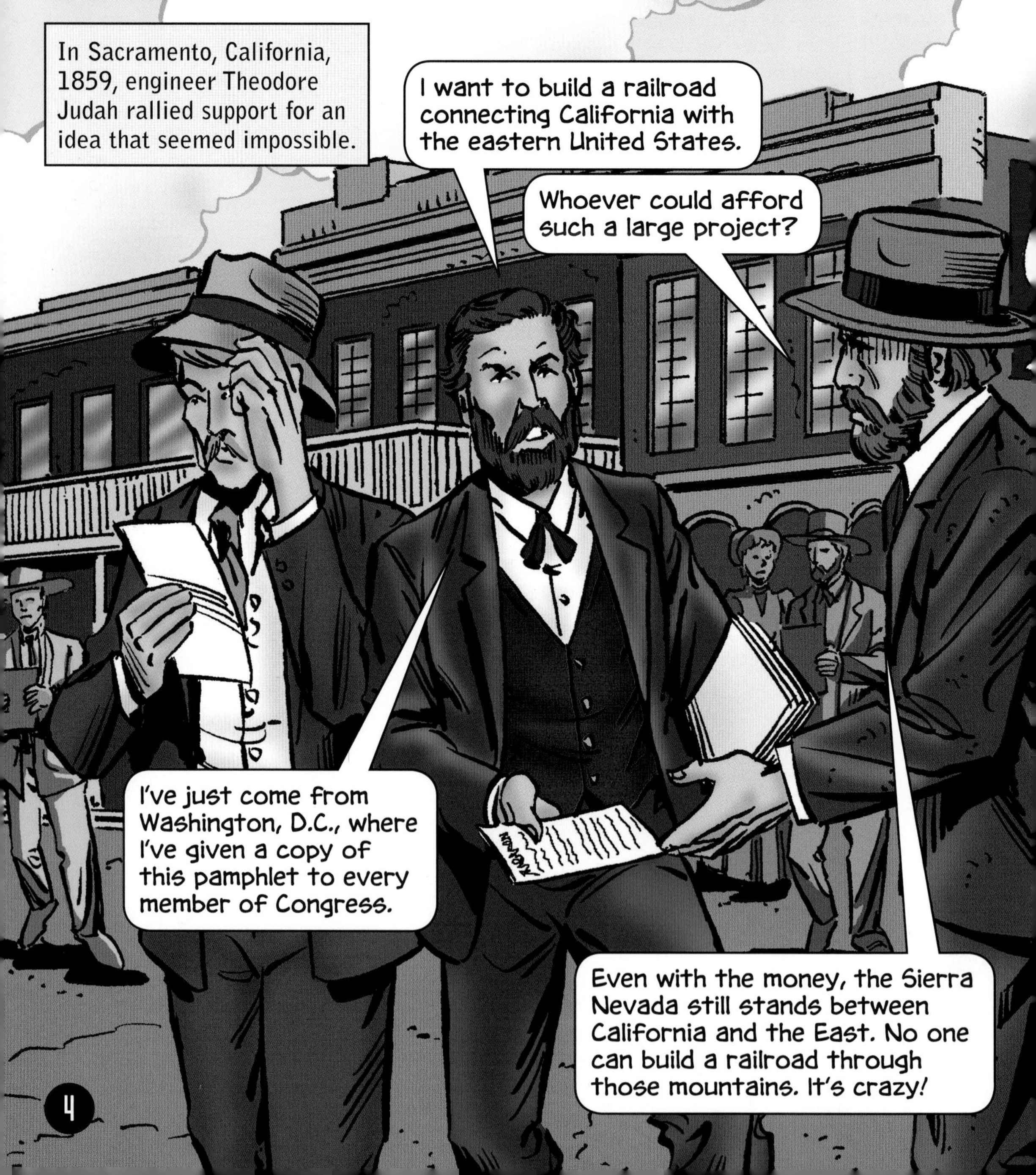

In Sacramento, California, 1859, engineer Theodore Judah rallied support for an idea that seemed impossible.
I want to build a railroad connecting California with the eastern United States.
Whoever could afford such a large project?
I've just come from Washington, D.C., where I've given a copy of this pamphlet to every member of Congress.
Even with the money, the Sierra Nevada still stands between California and the East. No one can build a railroad through those mountains. It's crazy!

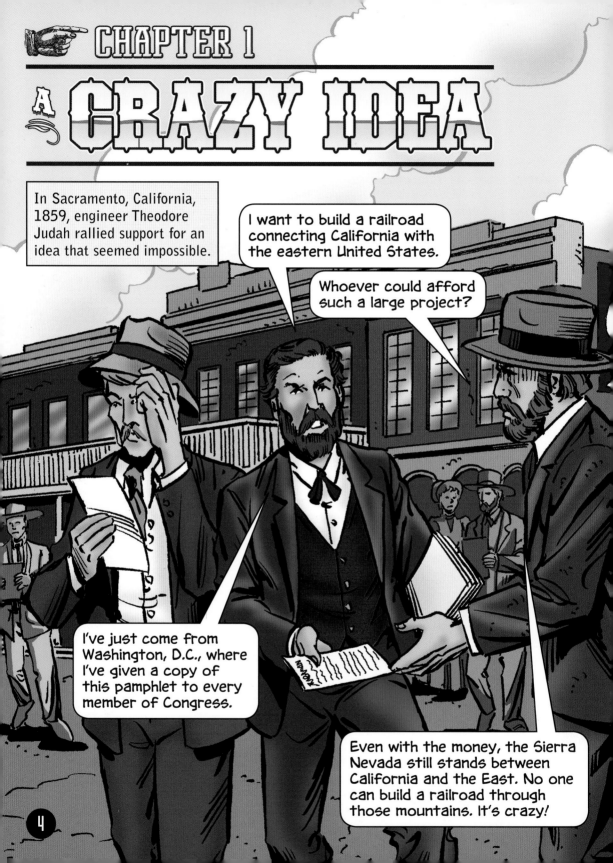

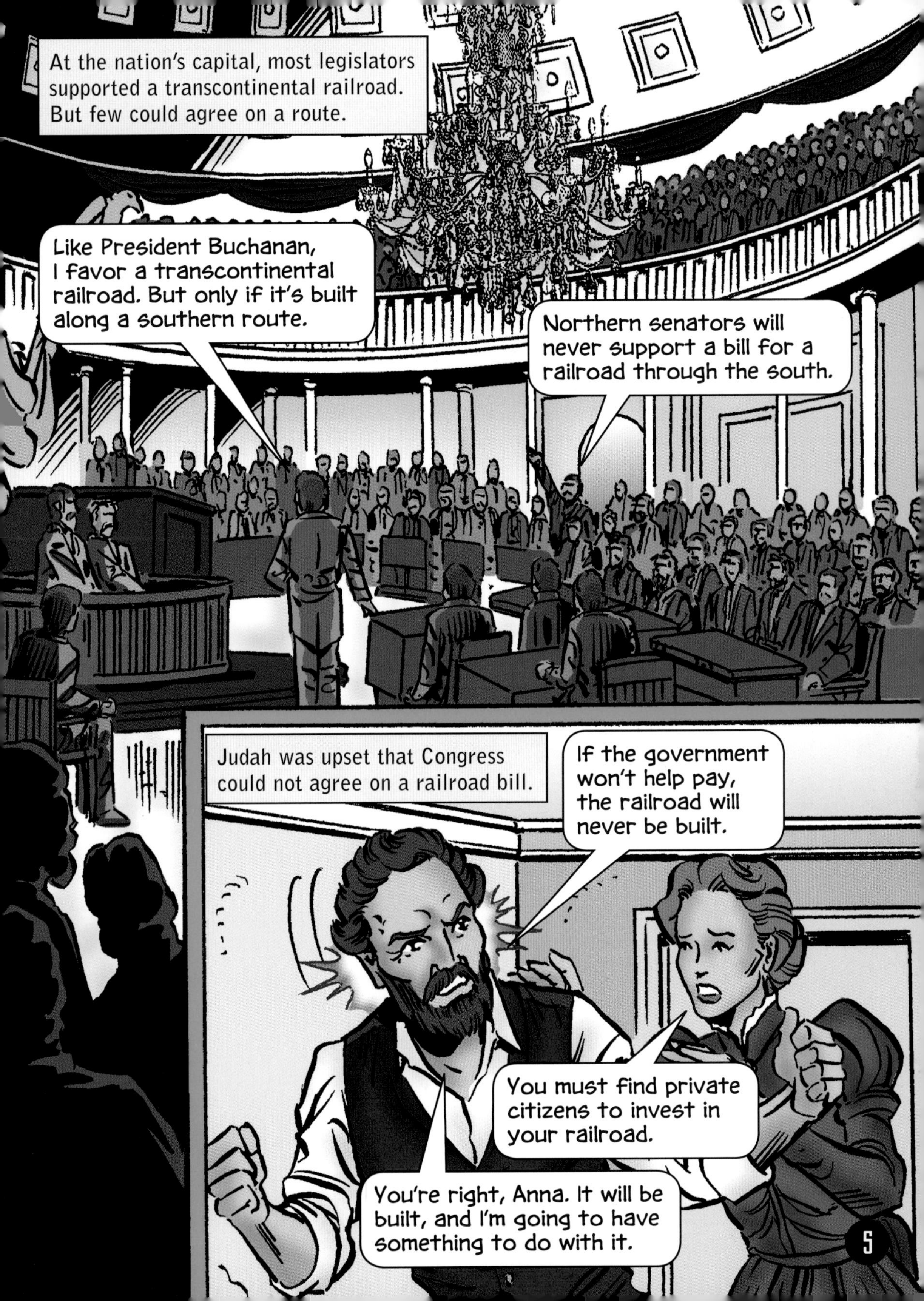
At the nation's capital, most legislators supported a transcontinental railroad. But few could agree on a route.
Like President Buchanan, I favor a transcontinental railroad. But only if it's built along a southern route.
Northern senators will never support a bill for a railroad through the south.
Judah was upset that Congress could not agree on a railroad bill.
If the government won't help pay, the railroad will never be built.
You must find private citizens to invest in your railroad.
You're right, Anna. It will be built, and I'm going to have something to do with it.

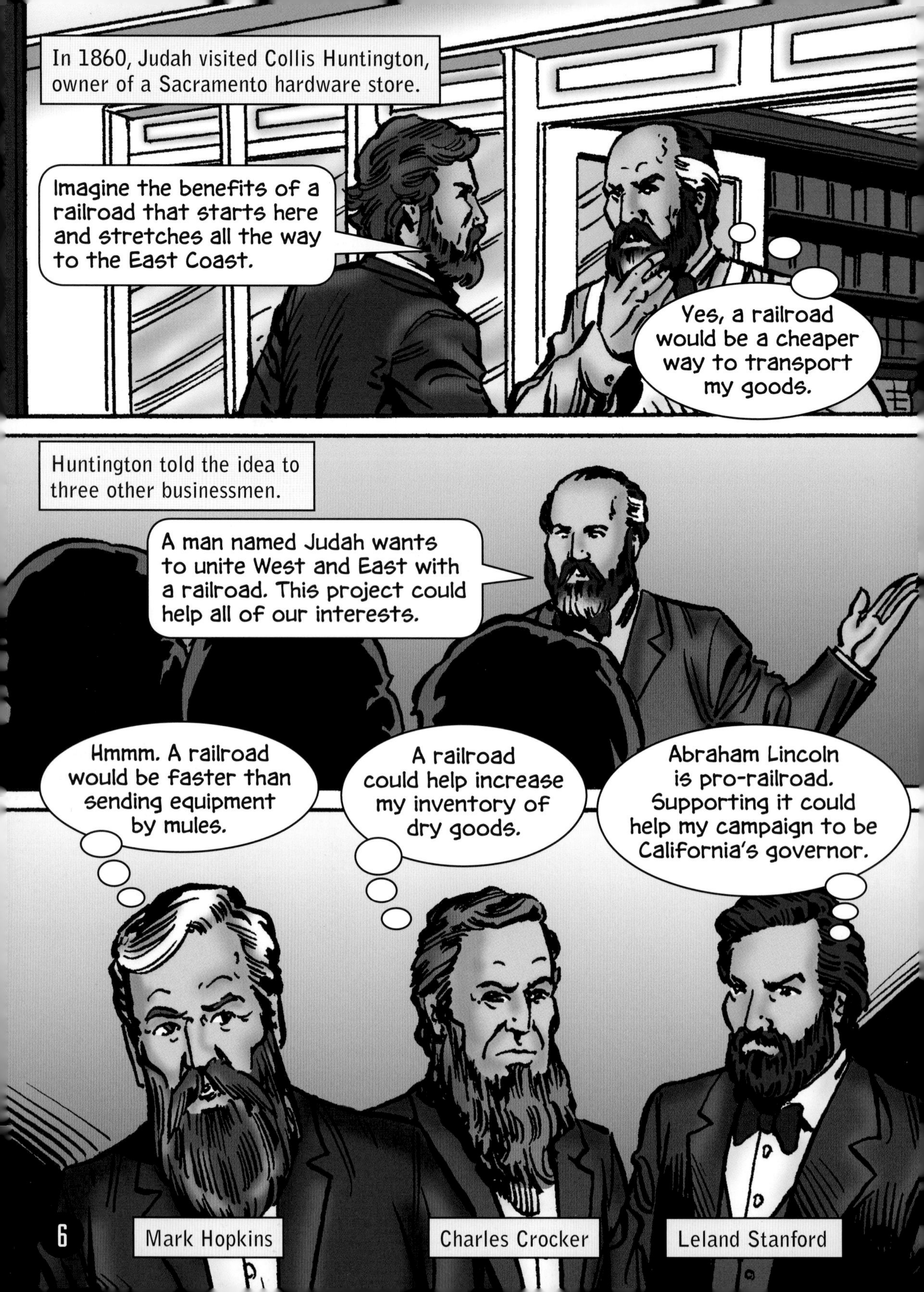
In 1860, Judah visited Collis Huntington, owner of a Sacramento hardware store.
Imagine the benefits of a railroad that starts here and stretches all the way to the East Coast.
Yes, a railroad would be a cheaper way to transport my goods.
Huntington told the idea to three other businessmen.
A man named Judah wants to unite West and East with a railroad. This project could help all of our interests.
Hmmm. A railroad would be faster than sending equipment by mules.
A railroad could help increase my inventory of dry goods.
Abraham Lincoln is pro-railroad. Supporting it could help my campaign to be California's governor.
Mark Hopkins
Charles Crocker
Leland Stanford

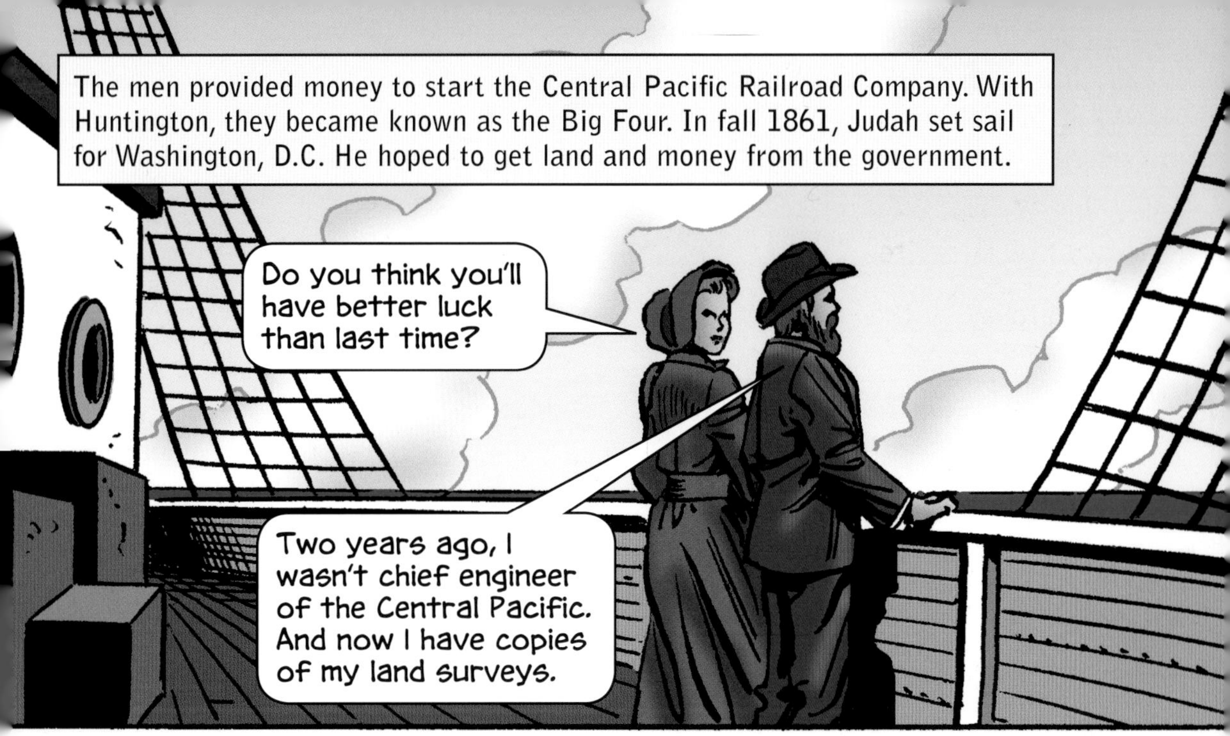
The men provided money to start the Central Pacific Railroad Company. With Huntington, they became known as the Big Four. In fall 1861, Judah set sail for Washington, D.C. He hoped to get land and money from the government.
Do you think you'll have better luck than last time?
Two years ago, I wasn't chief engineer of the Central Pacific. And now I have copies of my land surveys.

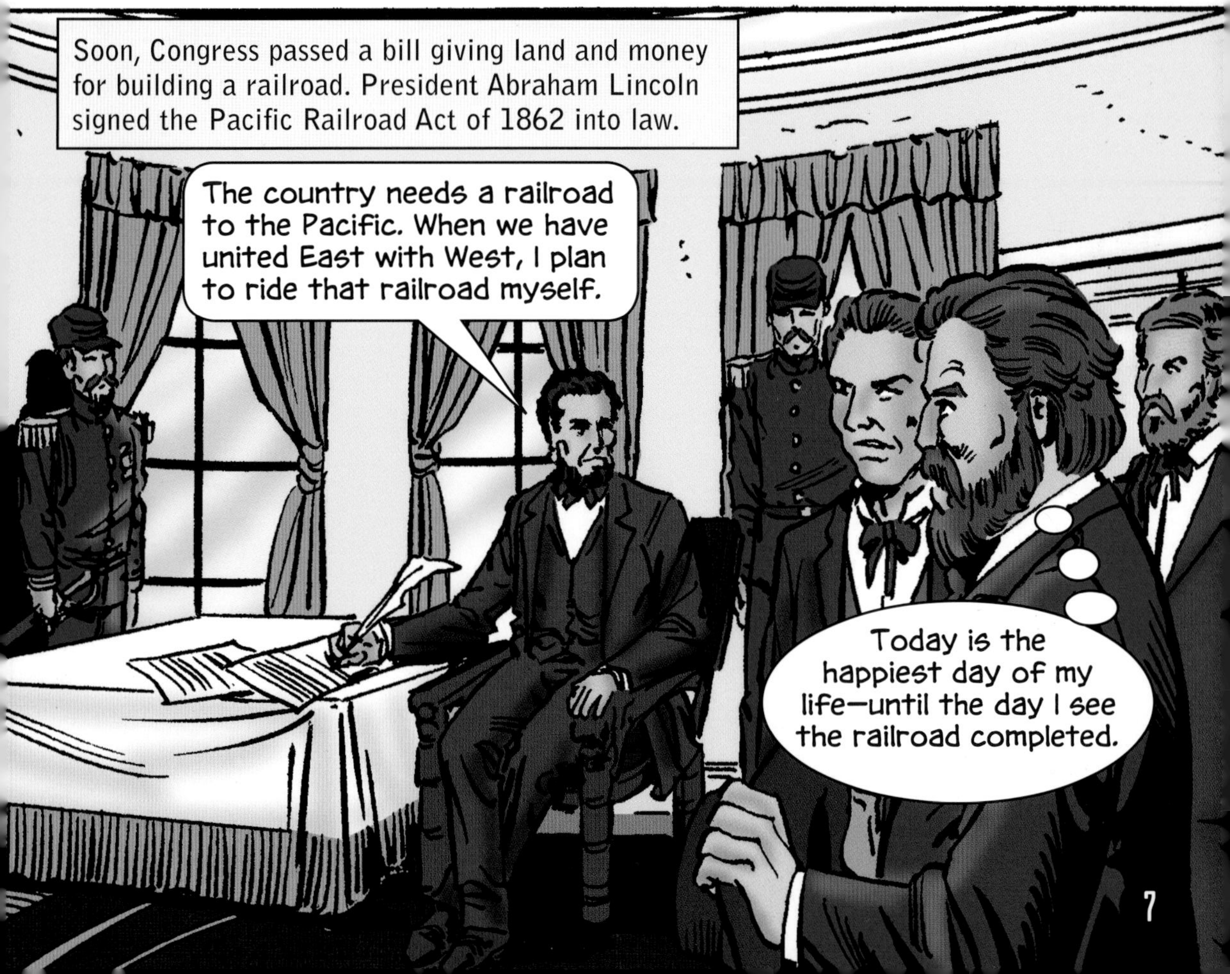
Soon, Congress passed a bill giving land and money for building a railroad. President Abraham Lincoln signed the Pacific Railroad Act of 1862 into law.
The country needs a railroad to the Pacific. When we have united East with West, I plan to ride that railroad myself.
Today is the happiest day of my life—until the day I see the railroad completed.

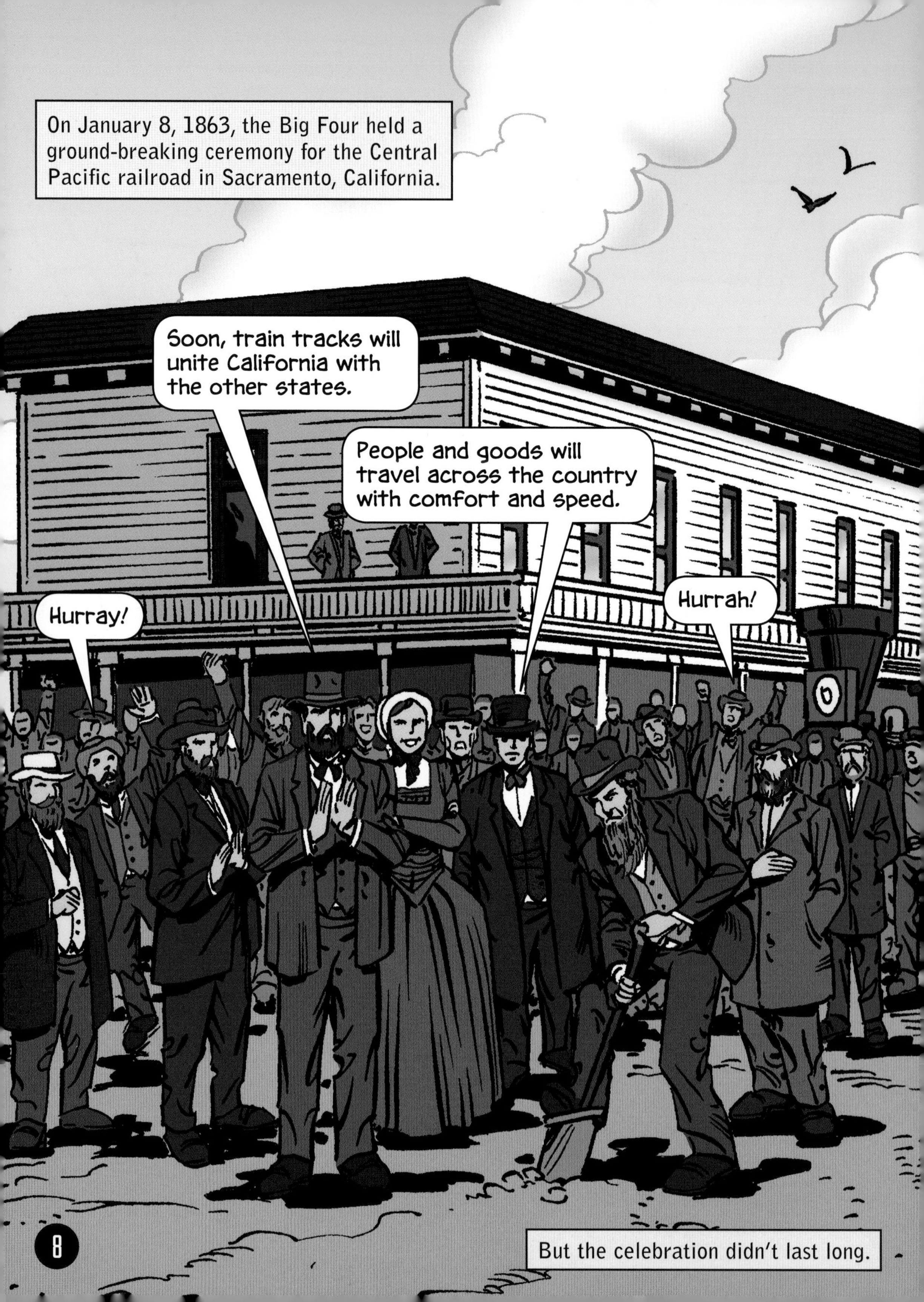
On January 8, 1863, the Big Four held a ground-breaking ceremony for the Central Pacific railroad in Sacramento, California.
Soon, train tracks will unite California with the other states.
People and goods will travel across the country with comfort and speed.
Hurray!
Hurrah!
But the celebration didn't last long.

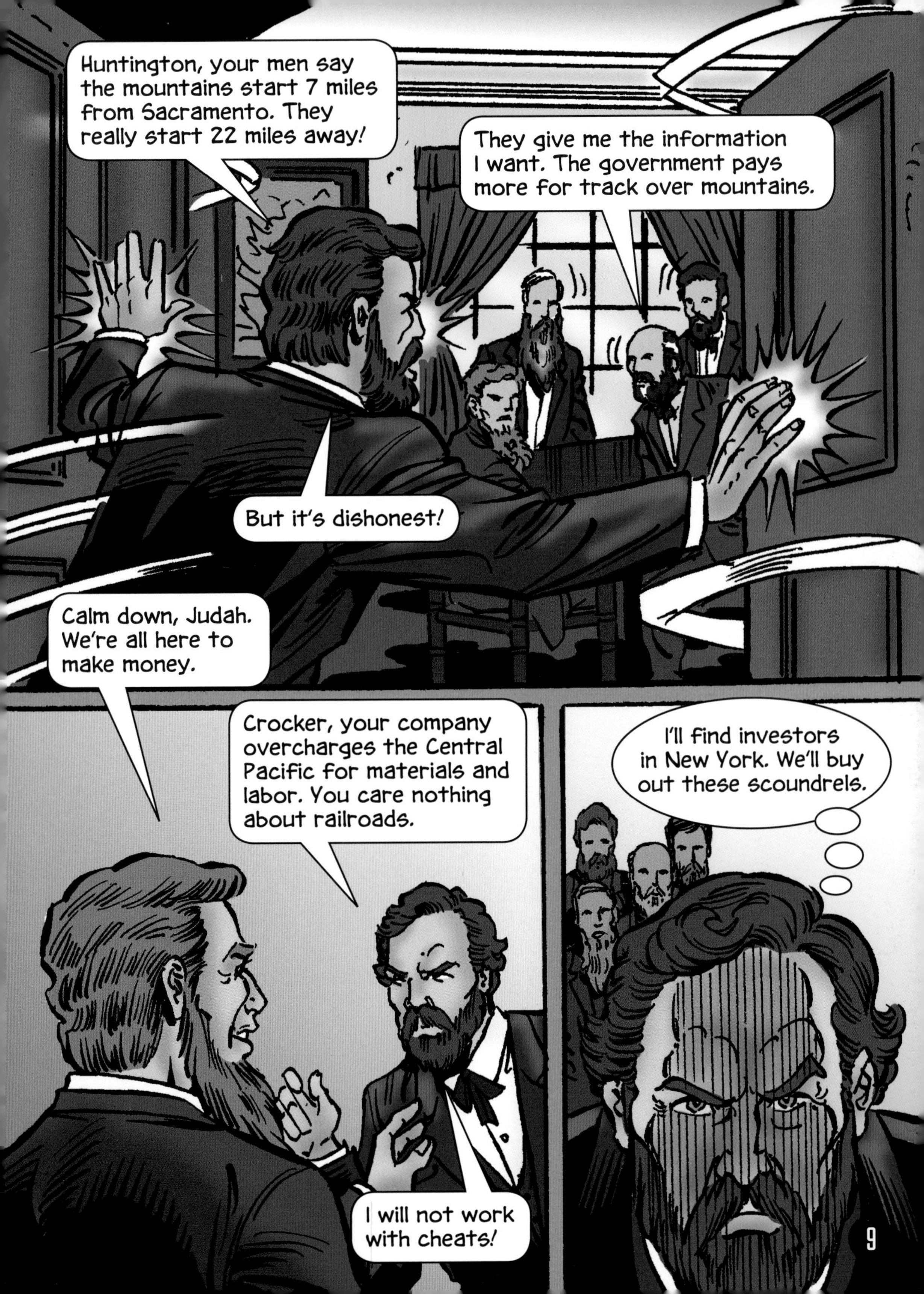
Huntington, your men say the mountains start 7 miles from Sacramento. They really start 22 miles away!
They give me the information I want. The government pays more for track over mountains.
But it's dishonest!
Calm down, Judah. We're all here to make money.
Crocker, your company overcharges the Central Pacific for materials and labor. You care nothing about railroads.
I will not work with cheats!
I'll find investors in New York. We'll buy out these scoundrels.

CHAPTER 2

THE CENTRAL PACIFIC

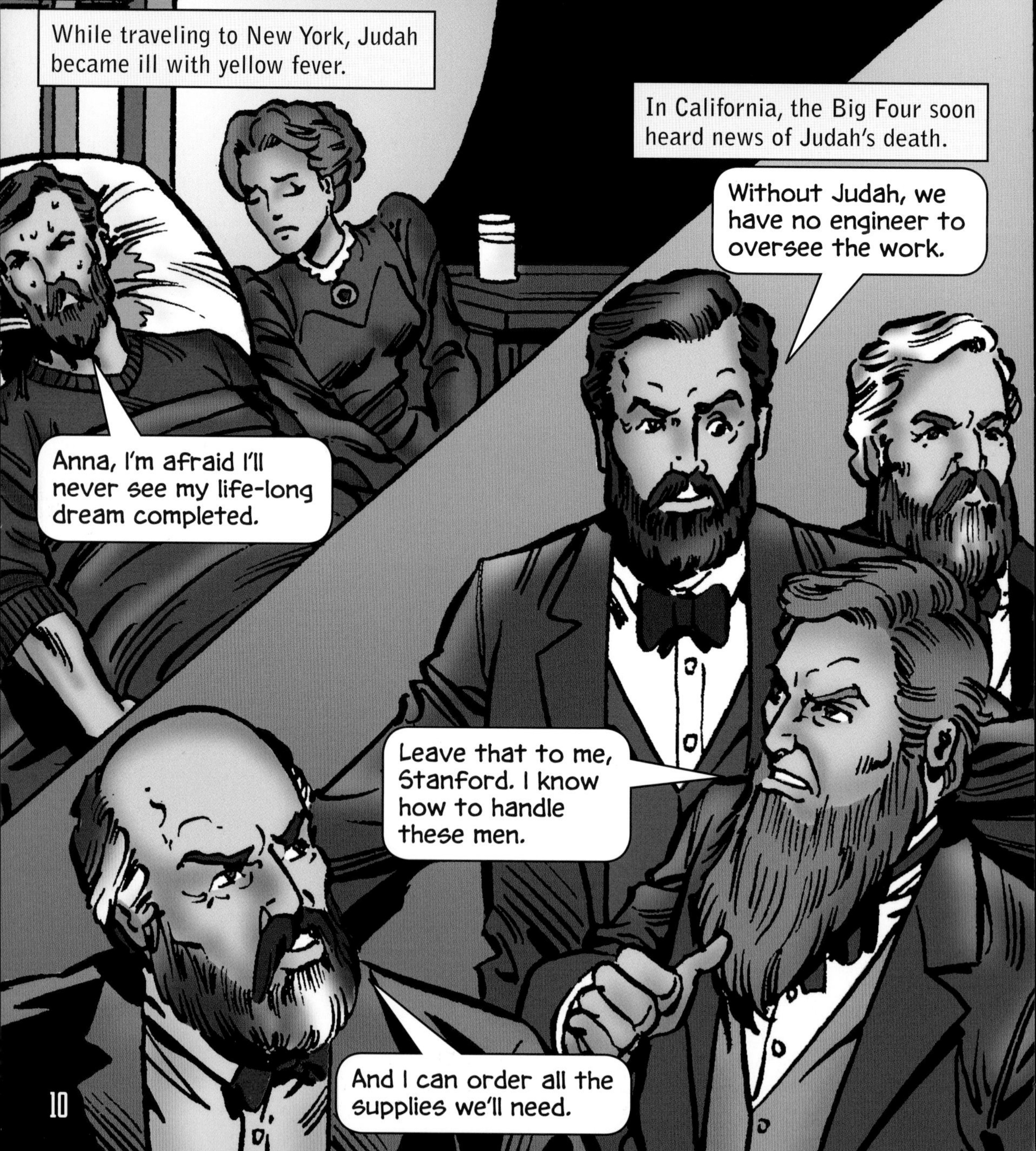

While traveling to New York, Judah became ill with yellow fever.
Anna, I'm afraid I'll never see my life-long dream completed.
In California, the Big Four soon heard news of Judah's death.
Without Judah, we have no engineer to oversee the work.
Leave that to me, Stanford. I know how to handle these men.
And I can order all the supplies we'll need.

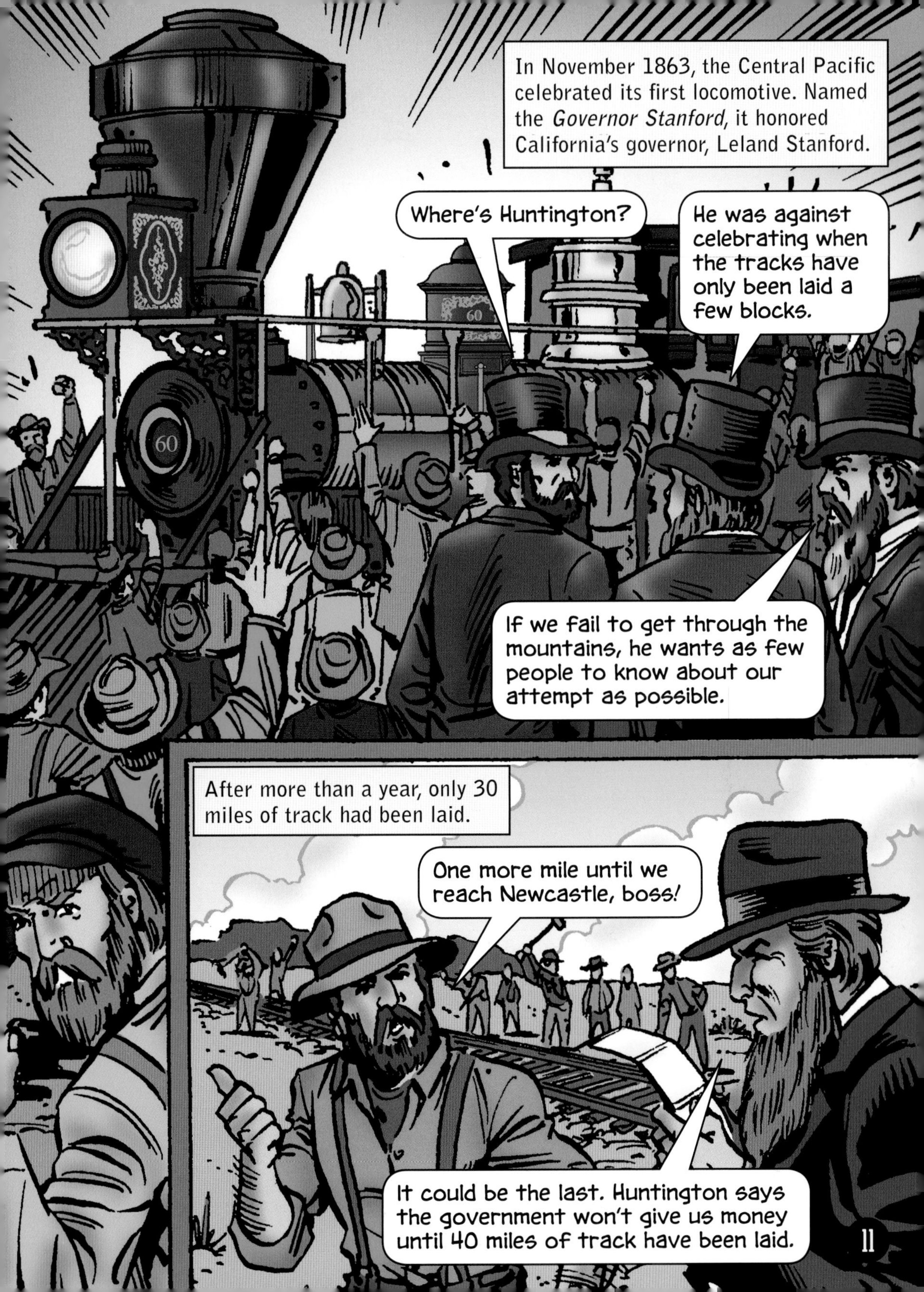
In November 1863, the Central Pacific celebrated its first locomotive. Named the *Governor Stanford*, it honored California's governor, Leland Stanford.
Where's Huntington?
He was against celebrating when the tracks have only been laid a few blocks.
If we fail to get through the mountains, he wants as few people to know about our attempt as possible.
60
After more than a year, only 30 miles of track had been laid.
One more mile until we reach Newcastle, boss!
It could be the last. Huntington says the government won't give us money until 40 miles of track have been laid.

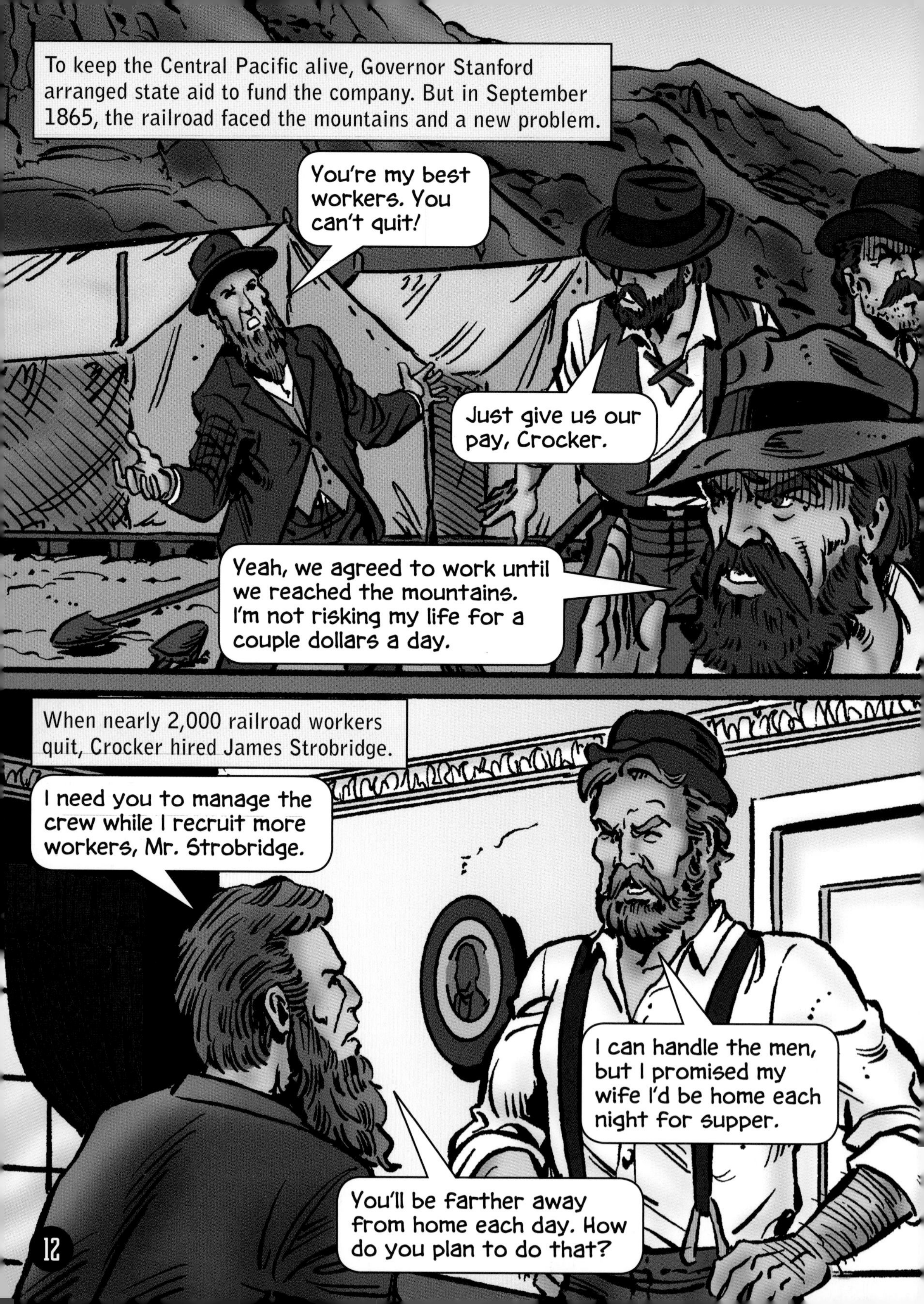

To keep the Central Pacific alive, Governor Stanford arranged state aid to fund the company. But in September 1865, the railroad faced the mountains and a new problem.
You're my best workers. You can't quit!
Just give us our pay, Crocker.
Yeah, we agreed to work until we reached the mountains. I'm not risking my life for a couple dollars a day.
When nearly 2,000 railroad workers quit, Crocker hired James Strobridge.
I need you to manage the crew while I recruit more workers, Mr. Strobridge.
I can handle the men, but I promised my wife I'd be home each night for supper.
You'll be farther away from home each day. How do you plan to do that?

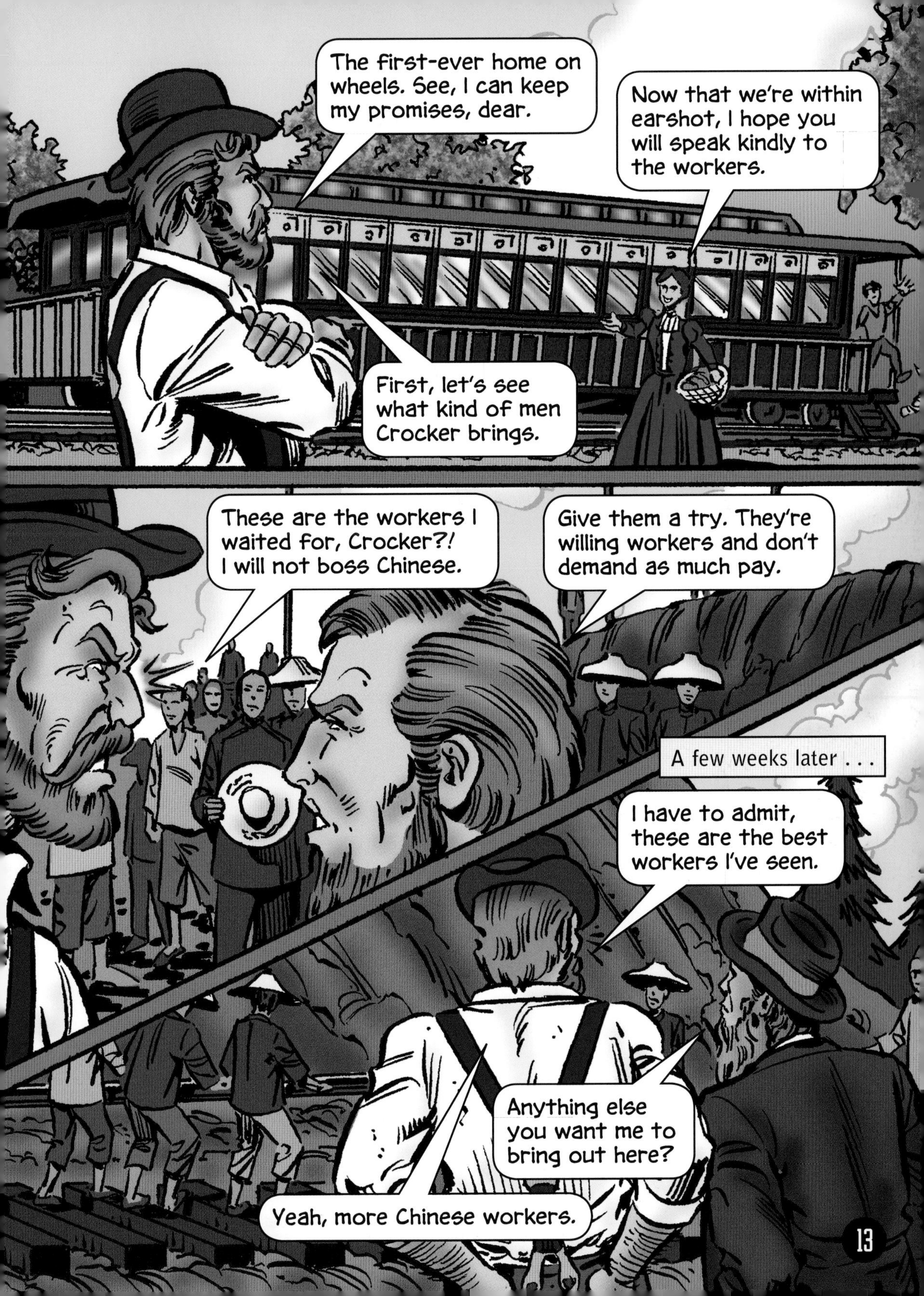
The first-ever home on wheels. See, I can keep my promises, dear.
Now that we're within earshot, I hope you will speak kindly to the workers.
First, let's see what kind of men Crocker brings.
These are the workers I waited for, Crocker?! I will not boss Chinese.
Give them a try. They're willing workers and don't demand as much pay.
A few weeks later . . .
I have to admit, these are the best workers I've seen.
Anything else you want me to bring out here?
Yeah, more Chinese workers.

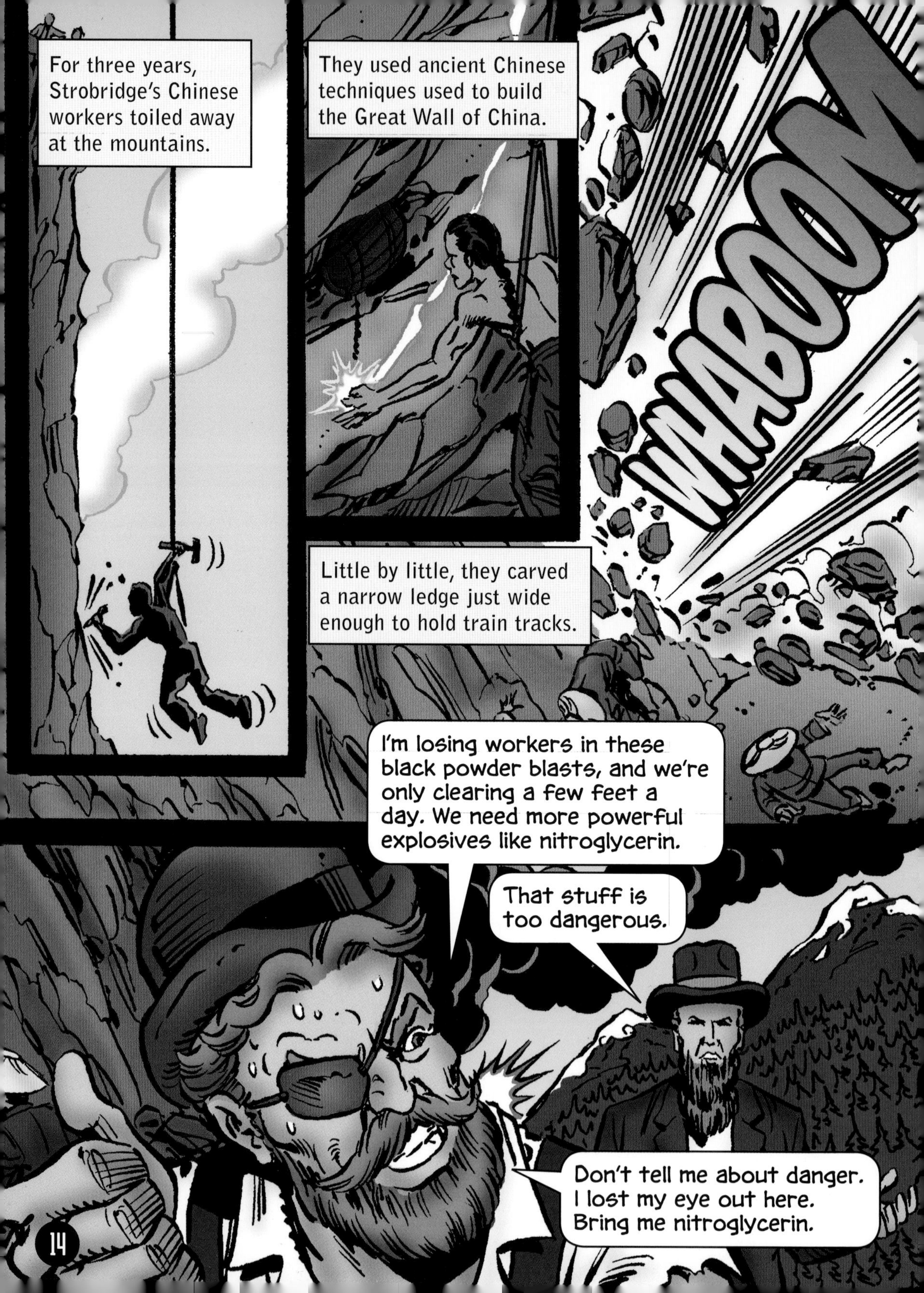
For three years, Strobridge's Chinese workers toiled away at the mountains.
They used ancient Chinese techniques used to build the Great Wall of China.
WHABOOM
Little by little, they carved a narrow ledge just wide enough to hold train tracks.
I'm losing workers in these black powder blasts, and we're only clearing a few feet a day. We need more powerful explosives like nitroglycerin.
That stuff is too dangerous.
Don't tell me about danger. I lost my eye out here. Bring me nitroglycerin.

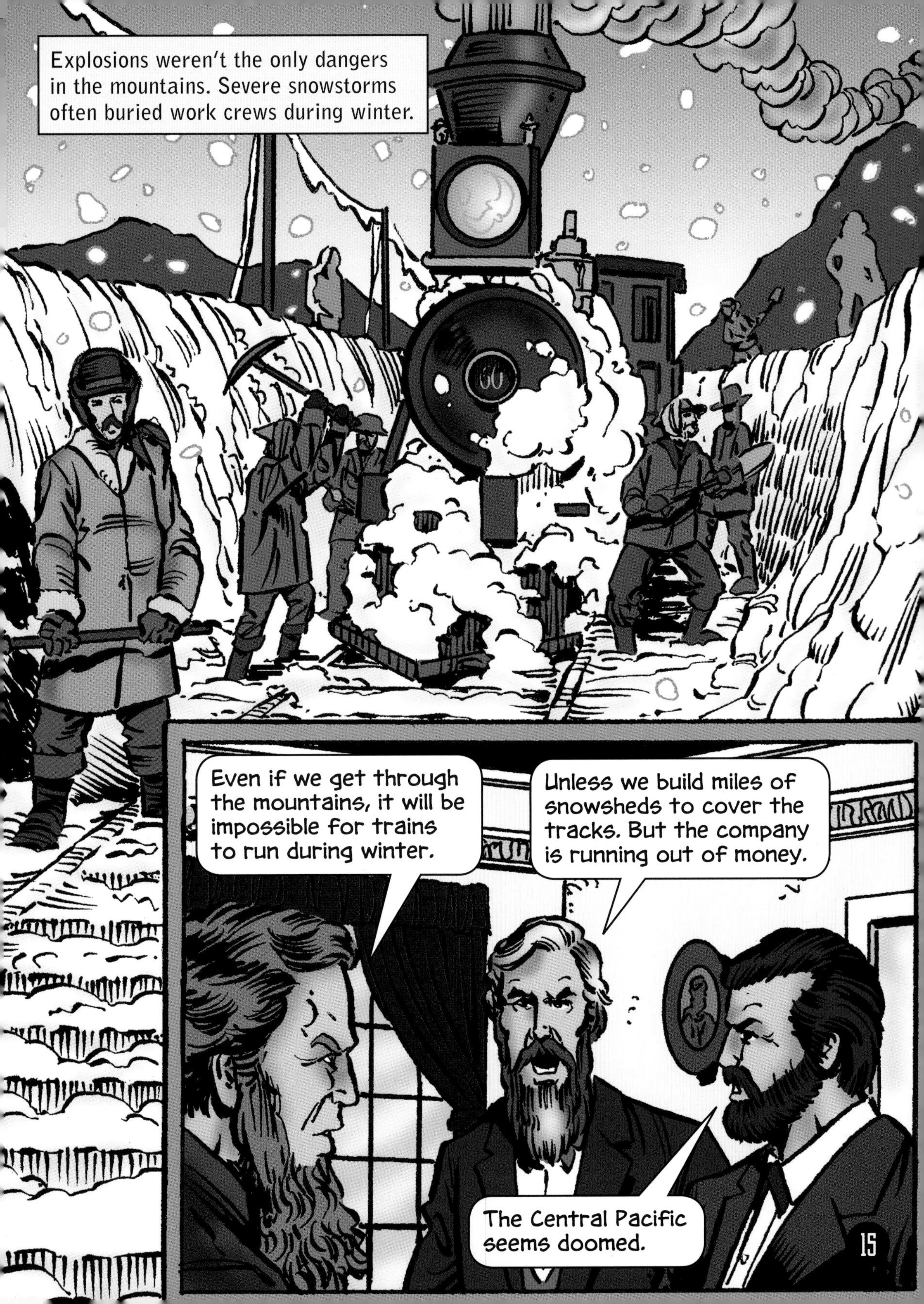
Explosions weren't the only dangers in the mountains. Severe snowstorms often buried work crews during winter.
60
Even if we get through the mountains, it will be impossible for trains to run during winter.
Unless we build miles of snowsheds to cover the tracks. But the company is running out of money.
The Central Pacific seems doomed.

CHAPTER 3

THE UNION PACIFIC

In Omaha, Nebraska, Thomas Durant headed up a different railroad company called the Union Pacific. They planned to start in the east and head west, in the opposite direction of the Central Pacific. On December 2, 1863, crowds gathered for the ground-breaking ceremony.

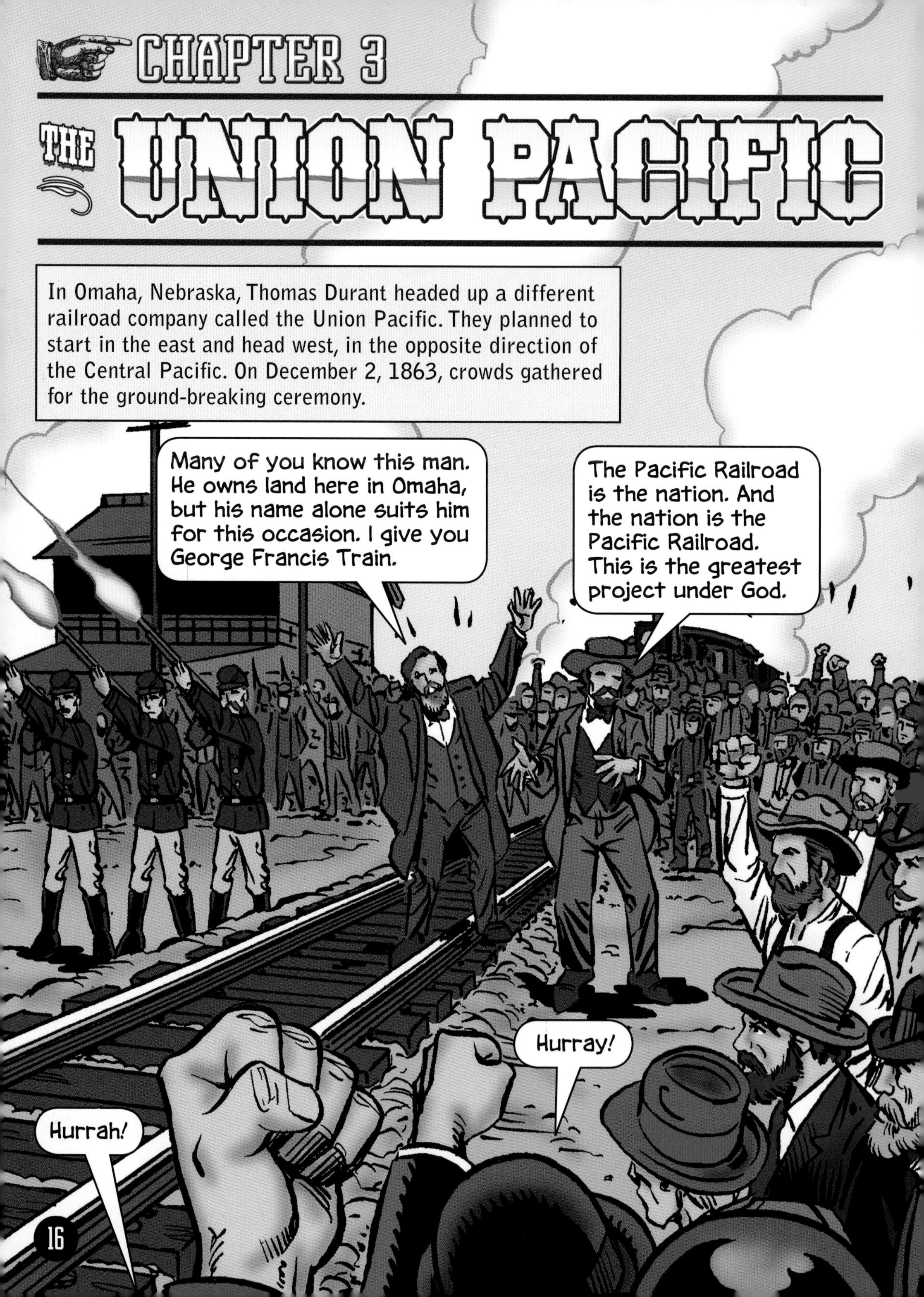
Many of you know this man. He owns land here in Omaha, but his name alone suits him for this occasion. I give you George Francis Train.
The Pacific Railroad is the nation. And the nation is the Pacific Railroad. This is the greatest project under God.
Hurray!
Hurrah!

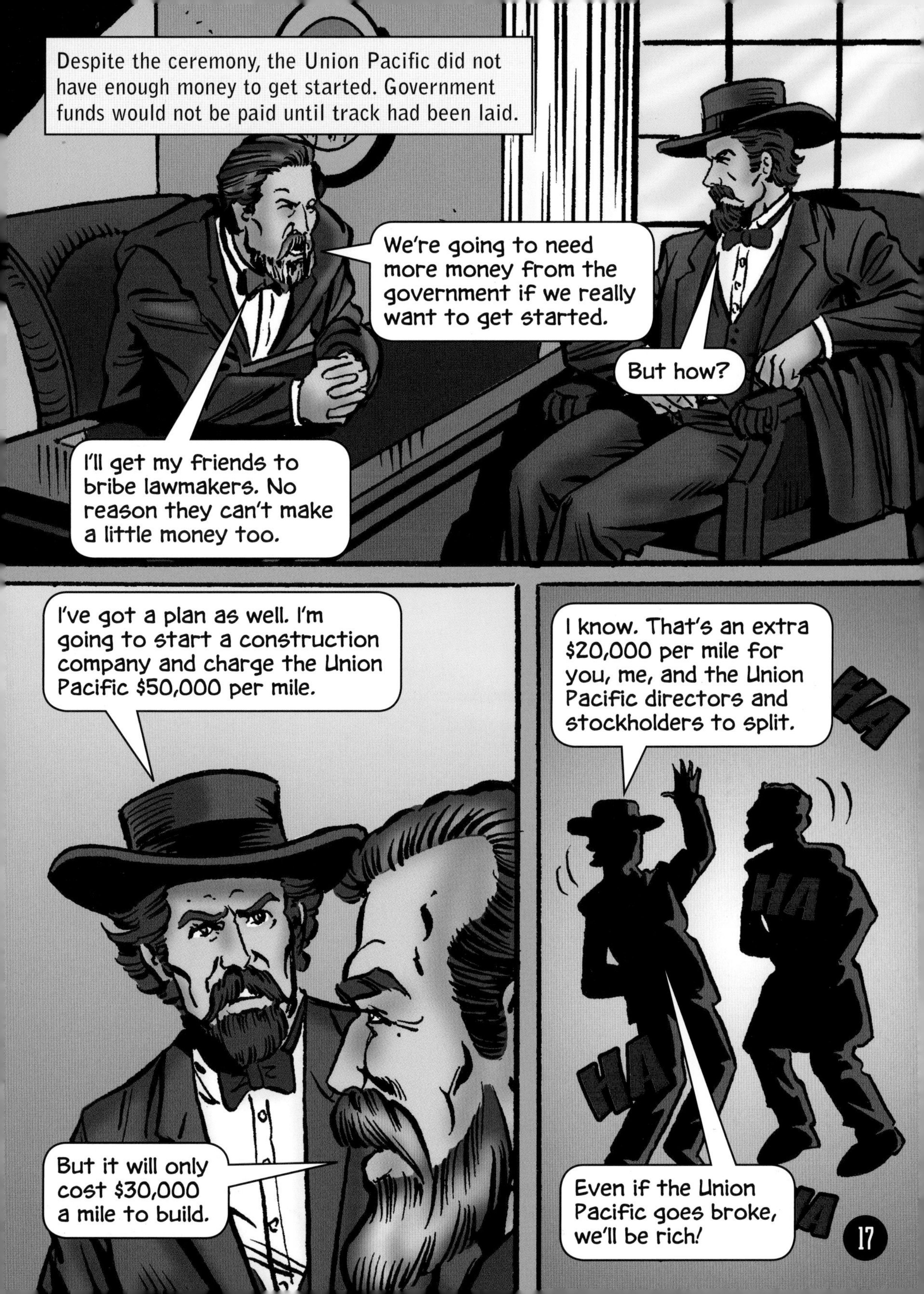
Despite the ceremony, the Union Pacific did not have enough money to get started. Government funds would not be paid until track had been laid.
We're going to need more money from the government if we really want to get started.
But how?
I'll get my friends to bribe lawmakers. No reason they can't make a little money too.
I've got a plan as well. I'm going to start a construction company and charge the Union Pacific $50,000 per mile.
But it will only cost $30,000 a mile to build.
I know. That's an extra $20,000 per mile for you, me, and the Union Pacific directors and stockholders to split.
HA
HA
HA
Even if the Union Pacific goes broke, we'll be rich!

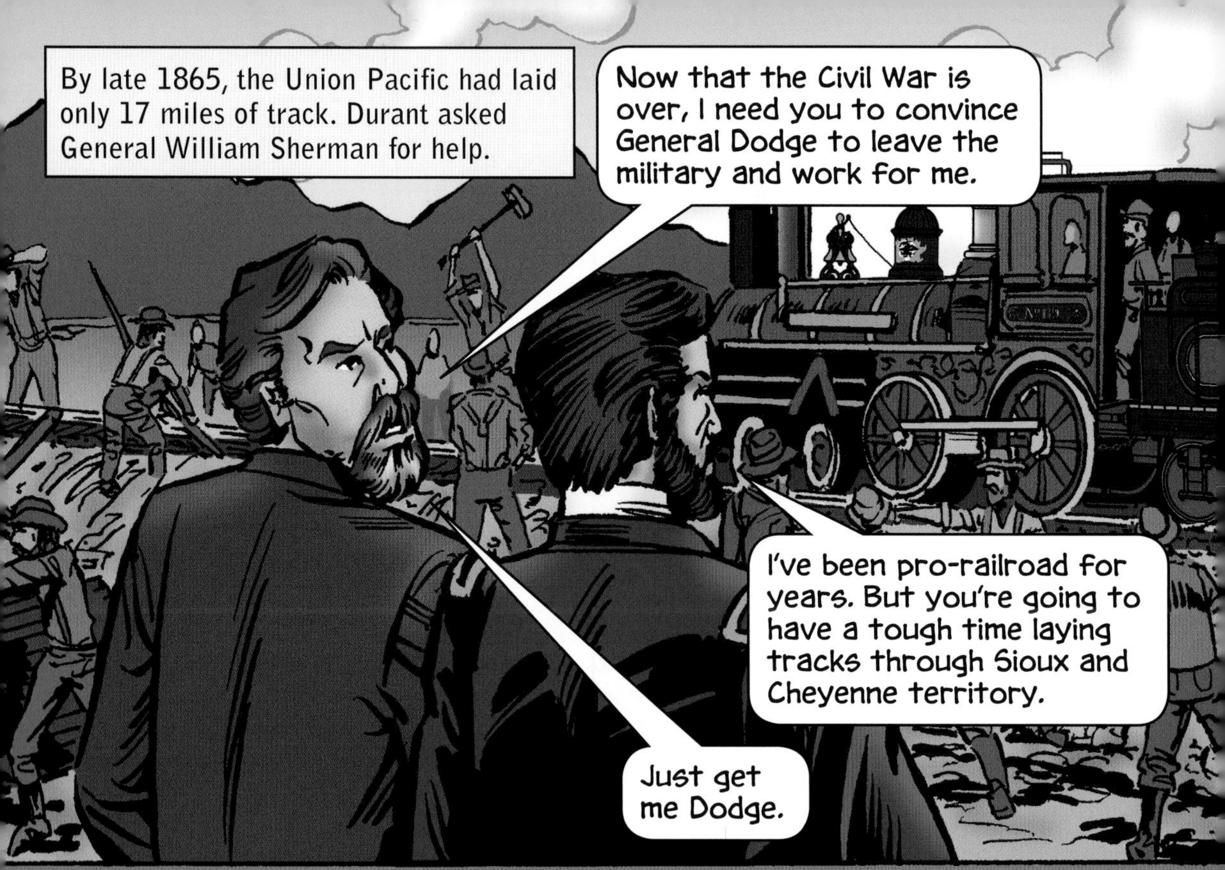
By late 1865, the Union Pacific had laid only 17 miles of track. Durant asked General William Sherman for help.
Now that the Civil War is over, I need you to convince General Dodge to leave the military and work for me.
I've been pro-railroad for years. But you're going to have a tough time laying tracks through Sioux and Cheyenne territory.
Just get me Dodge.

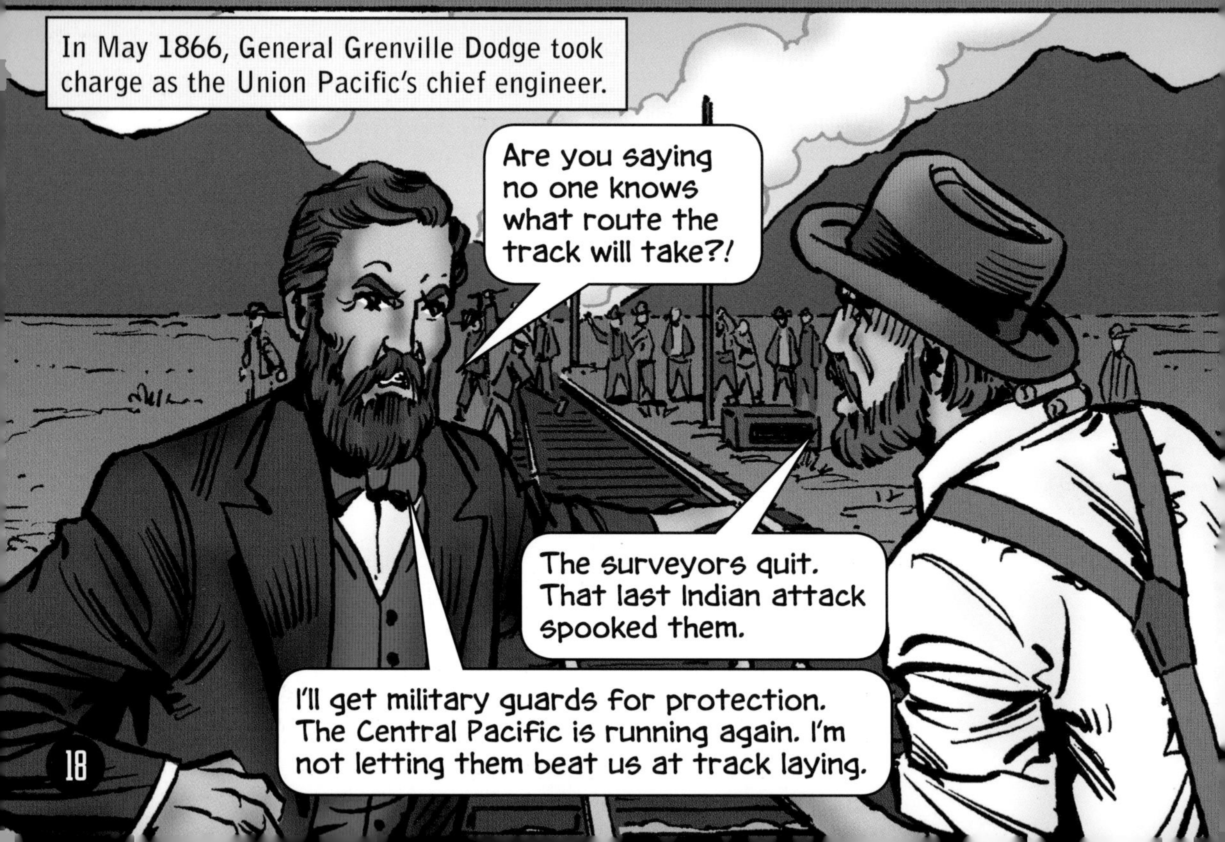
In May 1866, General Grenville Dodge took charge as the Union Pacific's chief engineer.
Are you saying no one knows what route the track will take?!
The surveyors quit. That last Indian attack spooked them.
I'll get military guards for protection. The Central Pacific is running again. I'm not letting them beat us at track laying.

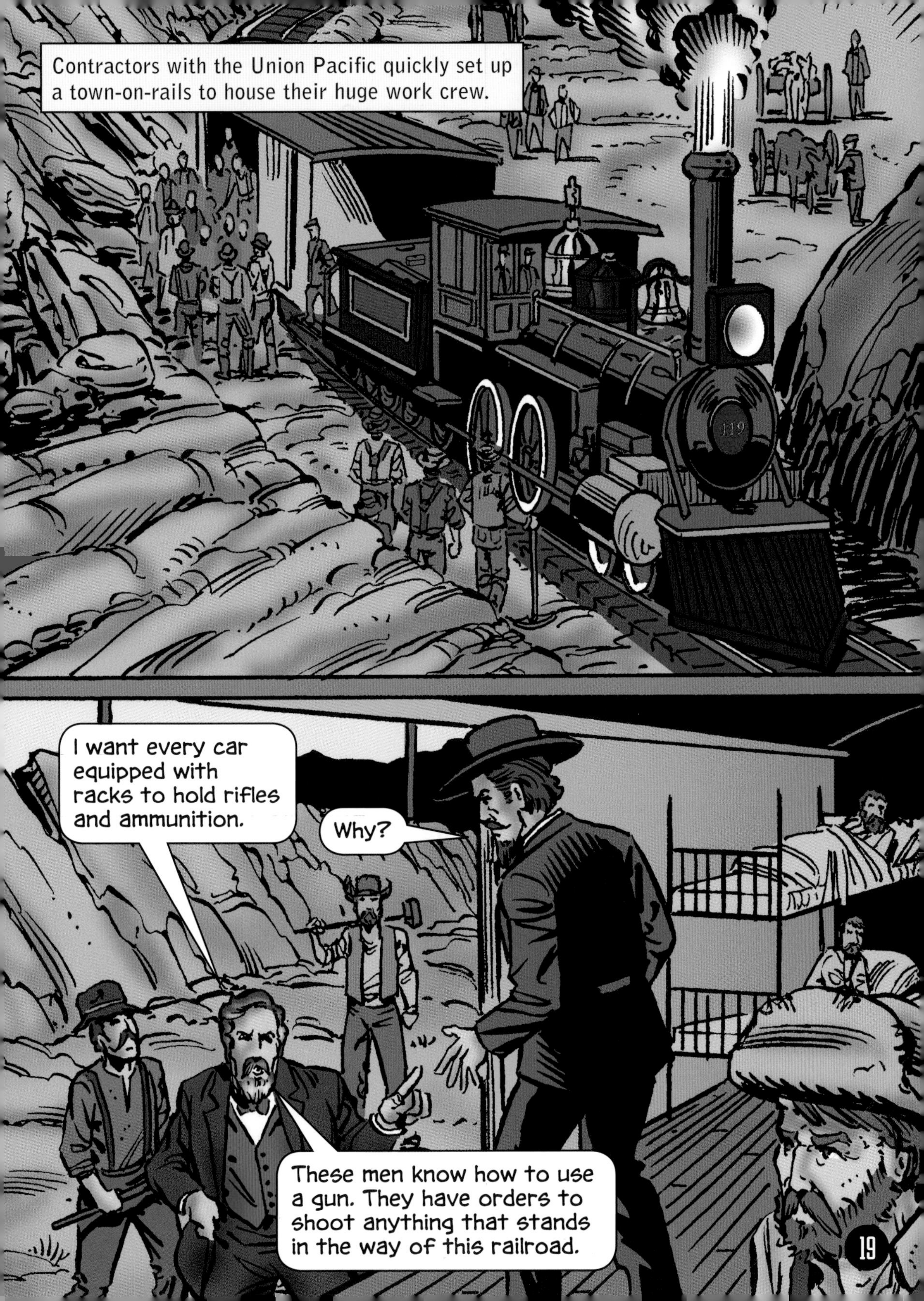
Contractors with the Union Pacific quickly set up a town-on-rails to house their huge work crew.
I want every car equipped with racks to hold rifles and ammunition.
Why?
These men know how to use a gun. They have orders to shoot anything that stands in the way of this railroad.

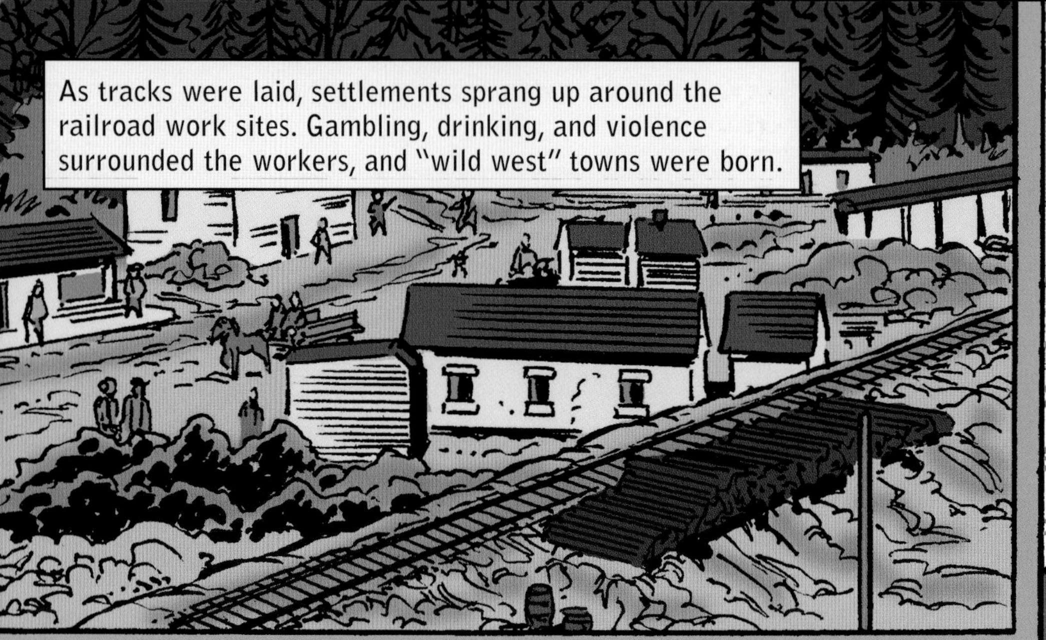
As tracks were laid, settlements sprang up around the railroad work sites. Gambling, drinking, and violence surrounded the workers, and "wild west" towns were born.

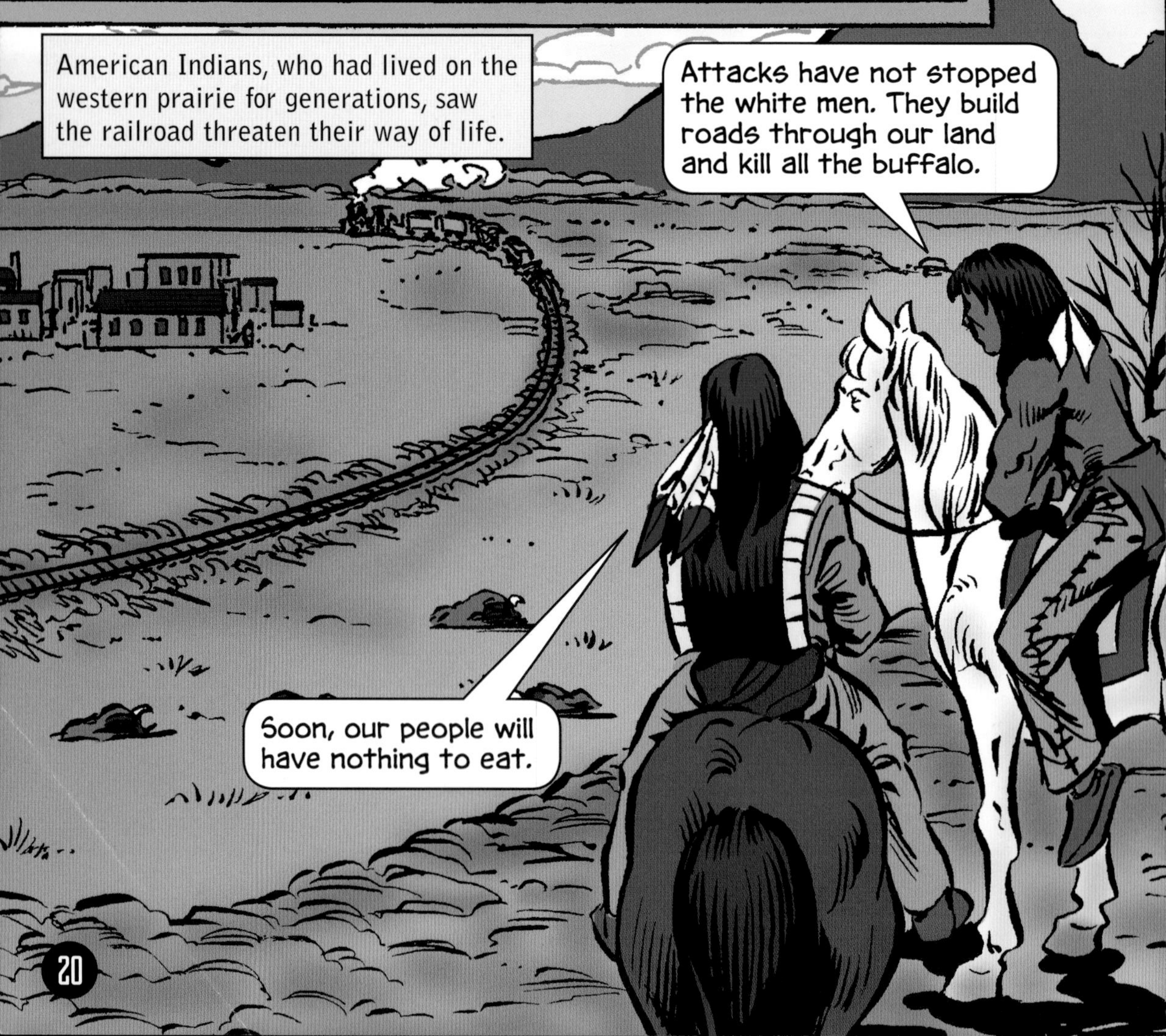
American Indians, who had lived on the western prairie for generations, saw the railroad threaten their way of life.
Attacks have not stopped the white men. They build roads through our land and kill all the buffalo.
Soon, our people will have nothing to eat.

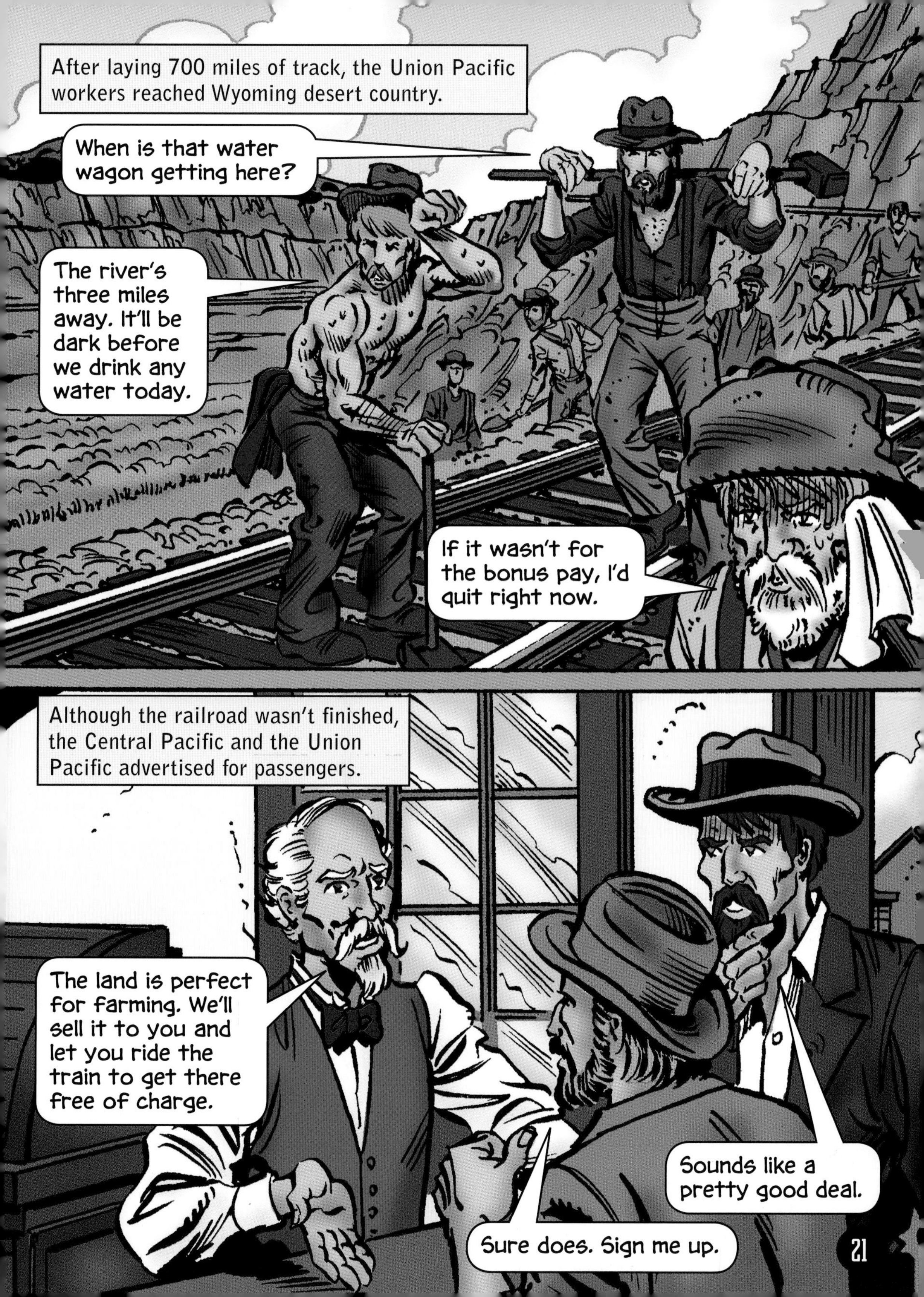
After laying 700 miles of track, the Union Pacific workers reached Wyoming desert country.
When is that water wagon getting here?
The river's three miles away. It'll be dark before we drink any water today.
If it wasn't for the bonus pay, I'd quit right now.
Although the railroad wasn't finished, the Central Pacific and the Union Pacific advertised for passengers.
The land is perfect for farming. We'll sell it to you and let you ride the train to get there free of charge.
Sounds like a pretty good deal.
Sure does. Sign me up.

CHAPTER 4

THE LAST SPIKE

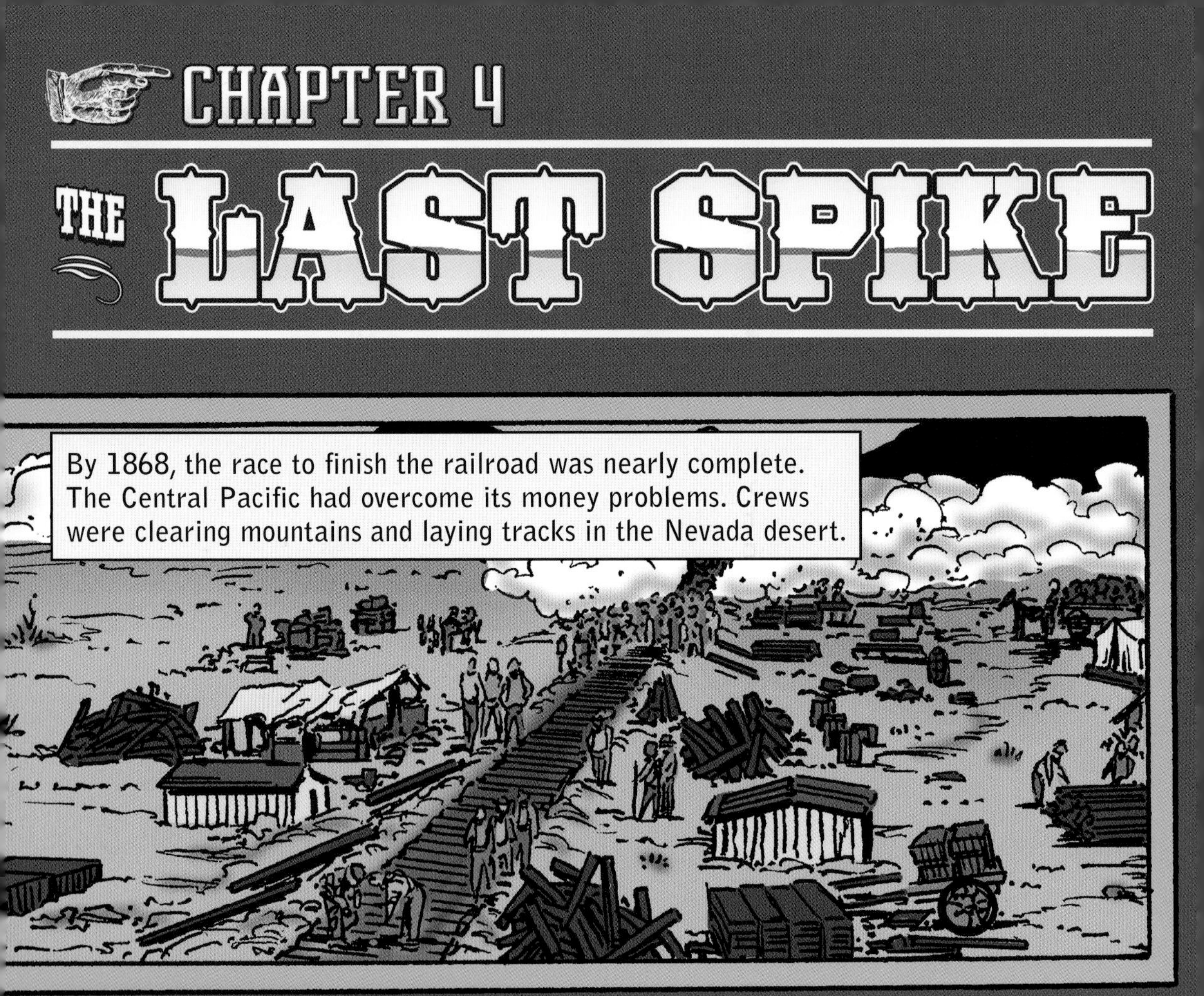
By 1868, the race to finish the railroad was nearly complete. The Central Pacific had overcome its money problems. Crews were clearing mountains and laying tracks in the Nevada desert.

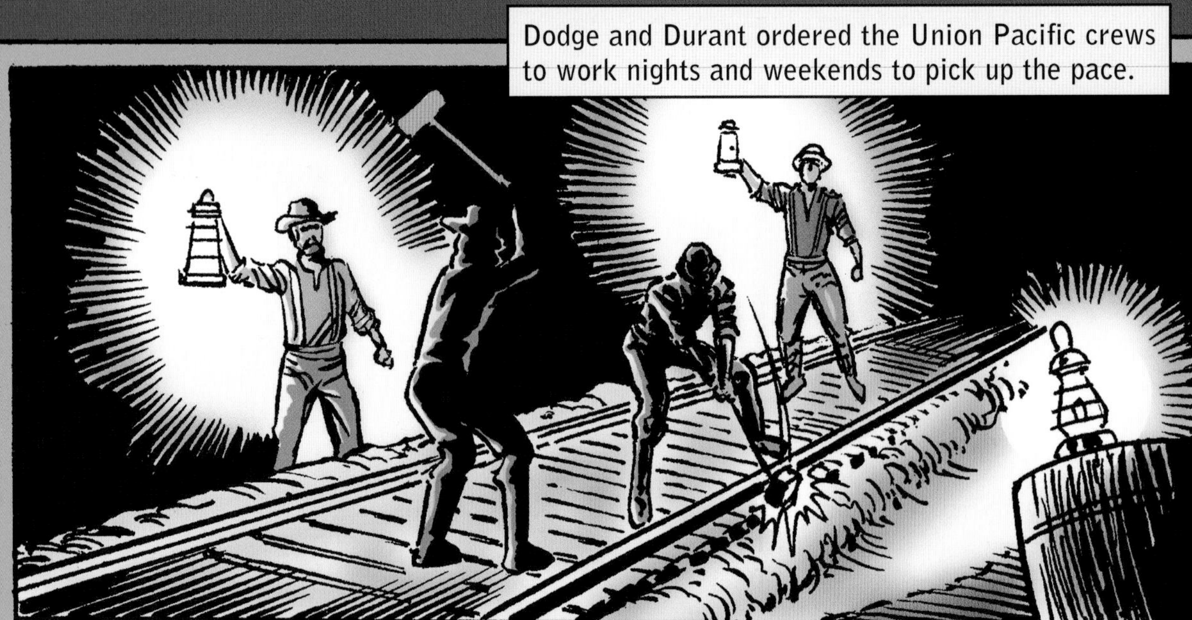
Dodge and Durant ordered the Union Pacific crews to work nights and weekends to pick up the pace.

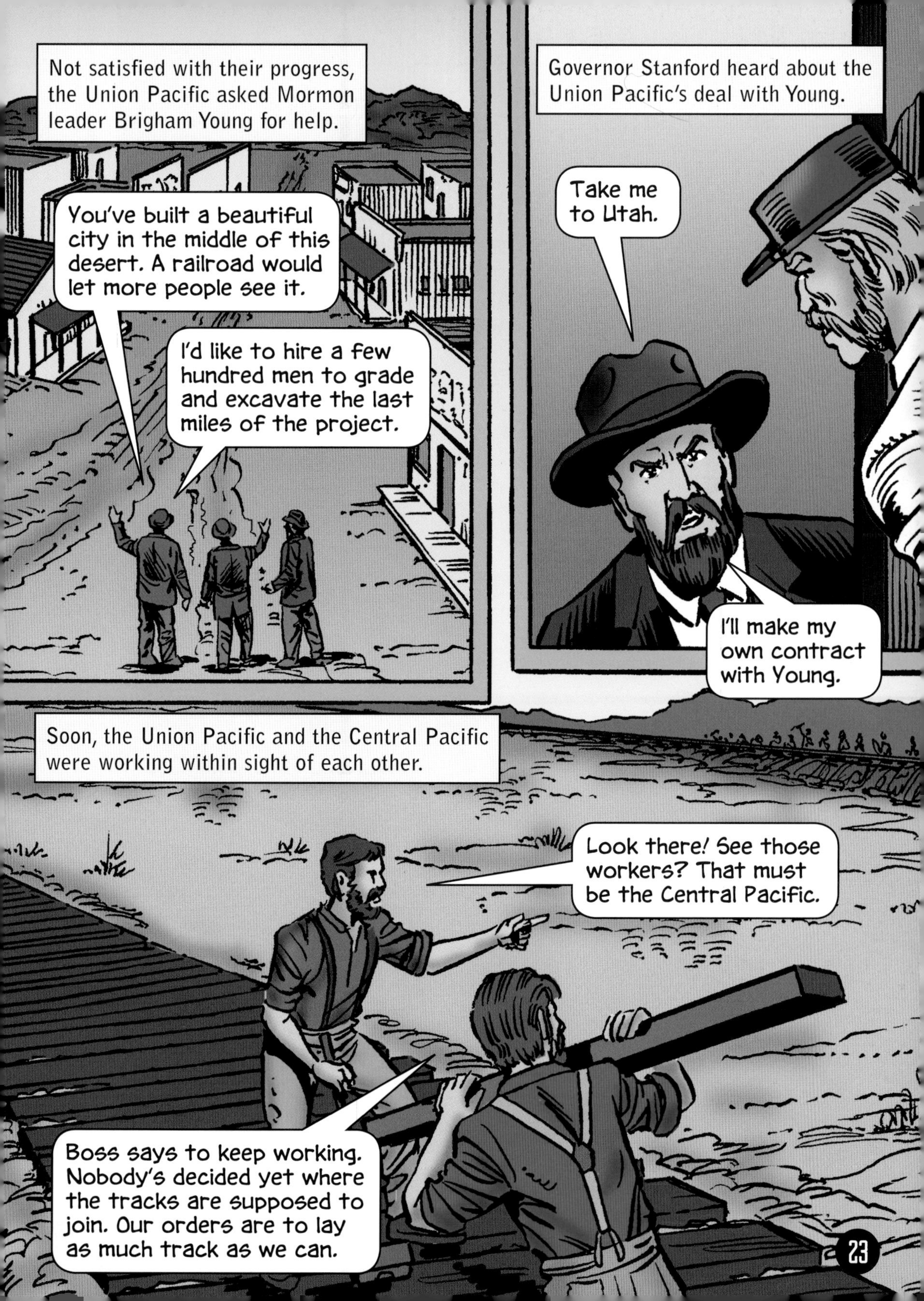
Not satisfied with their progress, the Union Pacific asked Mormon leader Brigham Young for help.
You've built a beautiful city in the middle of this desert. A railroad would let more people see it.
I'd like to hire a few hundred men to grade and excavate the last miles of the project.
Governor Stanford heard about the Union Pacific's deal with Young.
Take me to Utah.
I'll make my own contract with Young.
Soon, the Union Pacific and the Central Pacific were working within sight of each other.
Look there! See those workers? That must be the Central Pacific.
Boss says to keep working. Nobody's decided yet where the tracks are supposed to join. Our orders are to lay as much track as we can.

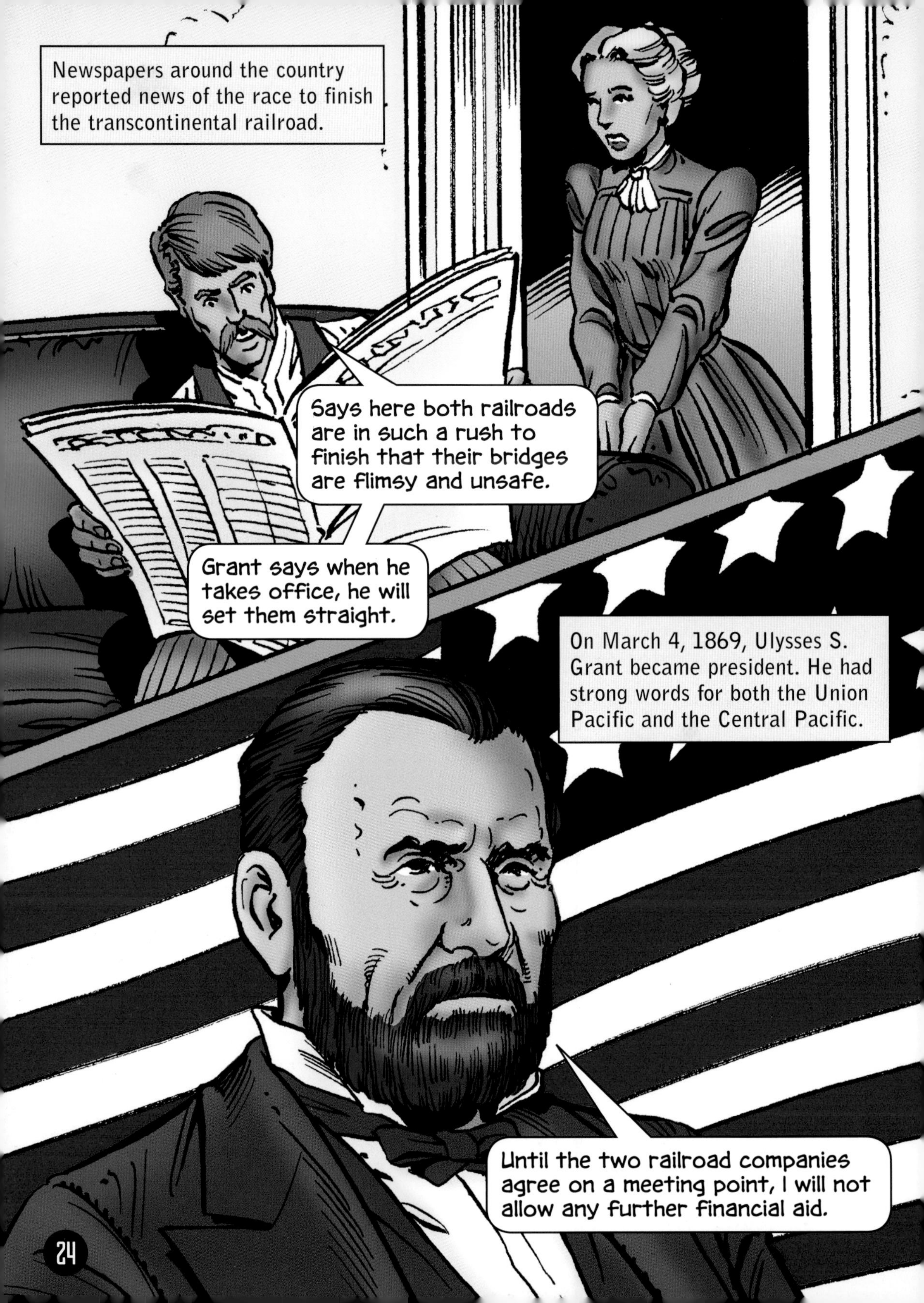
Newspapers around the country reported news of the race to finish the transcontinental railroad.
Says here both railroads are in such a rush to finish that their bridges are flimsy and unsafe.
Grant says when he takes office, he will set them straight.
On March 4, 1869, Ulysses S. Grant became president. He had strong words for both the Union Pacific and the Central Pacific.
Until the two railroad companies agree on a meeting point, I will not allow any further financial aid.

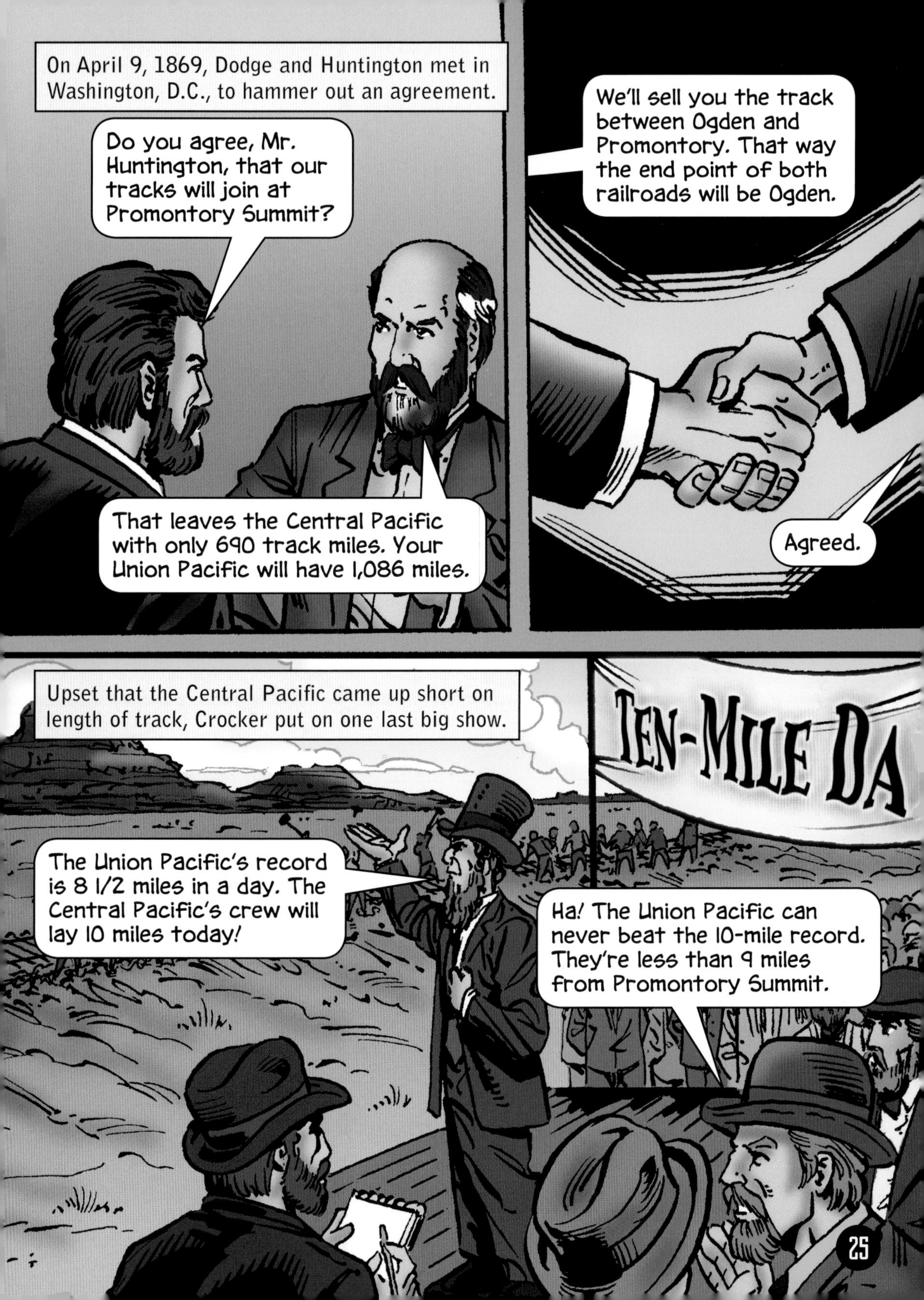
On April 9, 1869, Dodge and Huntington met in Washington, D.C., to hammer out an agreement.
Do you agree, Mr. Huntington, that our tracks will join at Promontory Summit?
That leaves the Central Pacific with only 690 track miles. Your Union Pacific will have 1,086 miles.
We'll sell you the track between Ogden and Promontory. That way the end point of both railroads will be Ogden.
Agreed.
Upset that the Central Pacific came up short on length of track, Crocker put on one last big show.
TEN-MILE DA
The Union Pacific's record is 8 1/2 miles in a day. The Central Pacific's crew will lay 10 miles today!
Ha! The Union Pacific can never beat the 10-mile record. They're less than 9 miles from Promontory Summit.

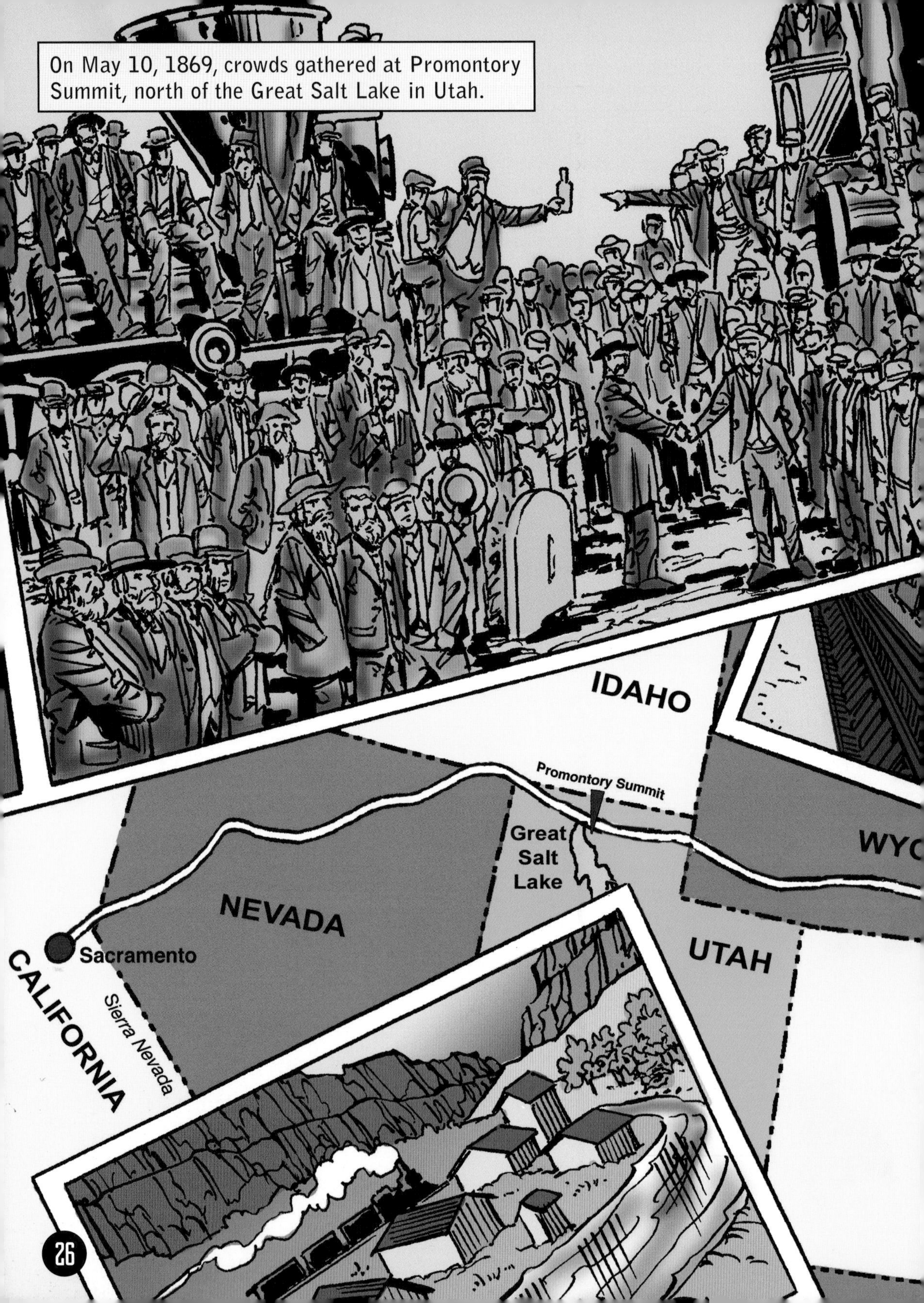

On May 10, 1869, crowds gathered at Promontory Summit, north of the Great Salt Lake in Utah.
IDAHO
Promontory Summit
Great Salt Lake
WYO
NEVADA
Sacramento
CALIFORNIA
Sierra Nevada
UTAH

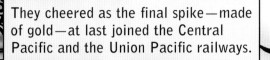

They cheered as the final spike—made of gold—at last joined the Central Pacific and the Union Pacific railways.

The Transcontinental Railroad changed the way Americans traveled and transported goods. A journey from coast to coast, which once took months, now took only a few days. In the years to come, Americans followed the railroad's tracks, settling the Great Plains and making the heartland their home.

DAKOTA

To Omaha

NEBRASKA

OLORADO

KANSAS

MORE ABOUT THE TRANSCONTINENTAL RAILROAD

☞ Although people called him Crazy Judah, Theodore Judah was a well-educated engineer. At 25, Judah was responsible for building the Niagara Gorge Railroad under Niagara Falls. Many doubted such a feat. Judah's success with this project convinced him a railroad through the Sierra Nevada to the eastern United States was possible.

☞ Chinese laborers were often paid less than other railroad workers. They also had to provide their own meals. One of their customs, drinking hot tea instead of water, kept the Chinese from getting sick. White workers drank unclean water from nearby ponds and streams, but Chinese workers drank hot tea. Boiling the water killed the germs that caused others to get sick.

☞ Snow was one of many dangers workers faced building the railroad through mountains. During the winter of 1867–68, temperatures became too cold for horses to work. Chinese laborers had to pull three locomotives and 40 train cars for 15 miles during a blizzard that winter.

- Workers who built the Transcontinental Railroad invented some slang terms for each other. They often called an engineer a "hogger." A drifter who worked on the railroad was known as a "boomer." Track laborers were called "gandy dancers," and any man caught sleeping on the job was a "hay."

- Stories and paintings of the last spike ceremony suggest a single gold spike connected the Central Pacific with the Union Pacific. Actually, there were four spikes for the ceremony. Two were made of gold from California, one of silver from Nevada, and the fourth made of iron, silver, and gold from Arizona. As soon as the ceremony was over, the gold and silver spikes were removed and replaced with regular iron spikes.

- A special train car was made for President Abraham Lincoln. Unfortunately, the only time Lincoln rode in the car was for his funeral. This elaborate coach brought Lincoln's body from Washington, D.C., to Springfield, Illinois, after he was assassinated in 1865.

- When the Transcontinental Railroad was finished, a first-class ticket from New York to San Francisco cost $136. Before the railroad, travelers spent about $1,000 and six months covering the same distance.

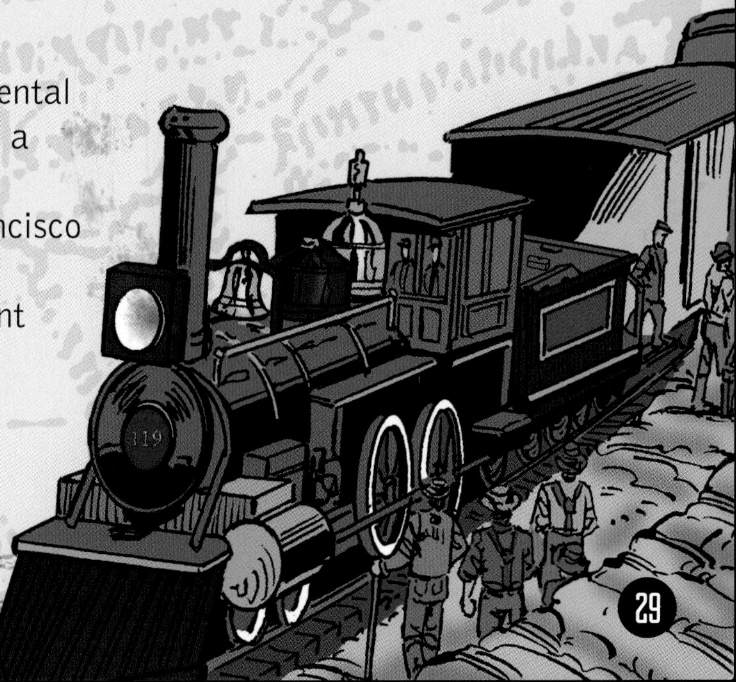

GLOSSARY

engineer (en-juh-NIHR)—someone trained to design and build machines, vehicles, bridges, roads, or other structures

excavate (EK-skuh-vate)—to dig in the earth

grade (GRAYD)—to make more level

legislator (LEJ-is-lay-tor)—a person elected to make or propose laws

locomotive (loh-kuh-MOH-tiv)—an engine used to push or pull railroad cars

nitroglycerin (nye-troh-GLISS-uhr-in)—an explosive liquid used to make very powerful explosions

INTERNET SITES

FactHound offers a safe, fun way to find Internet sites related to this book. All of the sites on FactHound have been researched by our staff.

Here's how:
1. Visit *www.facthound.com*
2. Choose your grade level.
3. Type in this book ID **0736864903** for age-appropriate sites. You may also browse subjects by clicking on letters, or by clicking on pictures and words.
4. Click on the **Fetch It** button.

FactHound will fetch the best sites for you!